T0354633

Nourishment
for the
Soul

A Guide to Well-Being

SHANNON N. JONES

BALBOA.PRESS
A DIVISION OF HAY HOUSE

Balboa Press books may be ordered through booksellers or by contacting:

Balboa Press
A Division of Hay House
1663 Liberty Drive
Bloomington, IN 47403
www.balboapress.com
844-682-1282

Print information available on the last page.

ISBN: 979-8-7652-2850-0 (sc)
ISBN: 979-8-7652-2851-7 (hc)
ISBN: 979-8-7652-2852-4 (e)

Library of Congress Control Number: 2022908456

Balboa Press rev. date: 06/01/2022

Contents

Acknowledgements ix
Preface xi

1   Just Be You 1
2   Walk It Out 3
3   A Dream or a Nightmare 5
4   Darkness Has No Power..7
5   Intuition..9
6   Shhh … 11
7   Problem vs. Solution 13
8   Synchronicity..15
9   Chill Out..17
10 What Kind of Driver Are You? 19
11 Savor Life 21
12 Imagine This...23
13 Moonshine 25
14 Lose to Win 27
15 Younique 29
16 The Five A's of Human Language 31
17 I Choose 33
18 Thank You..35
19 Extreme Sports...38

20 Lost and Found 41

21 Smiles 43

22 Juice Your Life 45

23 Don't Miss Your Season 47

24 Rain and Tears.. 49

25 Dear Teacher... 51

26 I Deserve to Be Known. I Deserve Friendship. 53

27 Attention = Focus = Energy 55

28 Stop, Drop, and Roll....................................... 57

29 Forgive Yourself.. 59

30 Egos vs. Eagles 61

31 Dinner 63

32 You Are Not What You Did............................ 65

33 Food Hall.. 67

34 Laugh Until It Hurts 69

35 Tap Out 71

36 Best Friends.. 73

37 Books Are My Friends 75

38 Mission Possible 77

39 A Balanced Life... 79

40 The Shutdown 81

41 Hidden.. 83

42 Don't Believe Everything You See 85

43 Live Your Values 87

44 Listen with the Heart 89

45 Contradictions 91

46 Opportunity.. 93

47 Blue Jay.. 95

48 Ordinary People Have Superpowers.................. 97

49 Don't Take It to the Grave 100

50 Love Me.. 102

51 Let It Go 104

52 Show Kindness Every Day 106

53 The Clay Talks to the Potter............................ 108

54	Stop, Rest, and Breathe	110
55	Three-Legged Dog	112
56	Dog Stuck in Mud	114
57	I Just Don't Know	116
58	Marinara Sauce	118
59	The Fixer-Upper	120
60	Surviving the In-Between	122
61	People Can't Give You What They Don't Have	124
62	Meditation Is My Best Friend	126
63	Serve Others	129
64	"Yet" Is a Chameleon	131
65	Cardinals Deliver Love Letters	133
66	We Learn What We Love, and We Love What We Learn	135
67	Ground Yourself	137
68	Abounding in Abundance	139
69	Visioning Exercise	141
70	Dogs "Tail" the Truth	143
71	The Rhythm of Life	145
72	Count Your Blessings	147
73	Never Mind the Place; Just Meditate	150
74	All Is "Well"	152
75	Ask for What You Want	155
76	Residing above the Clouds	157
77	Nature's Sound Bath Meditation	159
78	Illusions	161
79	Don't Trust What You See	163
80	All There Is to Know	165
81	I Choose My "I'm Too's"	167
82	Our Needs Are the Same, Just in Different Forms	170
83	Find or Create	172
84	My Needs Must Take Priority	174

Acknowledgements

I am deeply honored to be the proud mother of my two sons, Chance and Prince. They remind me daily of my strength and unknowingly reveal to me my potential. Prince served as my accountability partner, pushing me to publish this book. Chance provided the space for me to write uninterrupted.

It is because of them that this book is published as I knew that I could not tell them to pursue their dreams if I did not pursue mine. Their presence served as ongoing support and motivation to birth this book just as a mother gives birth to her newborn.

It is because of them that this book is living and breathing, and has come into your hands. Therefore, I can share this journey with you.

Thank you, boys!

Preface

Nourishment for the Soul: A Guide to Well-Being is a lyrical self-help guide filled with practical, concrete, and concise actionable advice even the busiest of readers can integrate into their daily lives. It is incredibly insightful and one of the best road maps for self-navigation. This guide fosters well-being to support a state of holistic health and harmony for the mind, body, and soul. This guide helps the reader explore well-being through mindfulness, self-love, self-awareness, and self-discovery. It captures the essence of hope, authenticity, and kindness.

Through mindfulness, we know that our minds can create and heal when it is given sufficient space to rest.

Through self-love, we learn to love ourselves and we teach others how to love us. When we learn to love ourselves, we become the protagonist and hero of our own love story.

Through self-awareness, we become the observants of our lives and are fully aware of ourselves, our thoughts and emotions, strengths, and limitations to create harmony and alignment within our internal and external worlds. This is the art of self-mastery.

Through self-discovery, we discover our talents, gifts, and true selves. The journey of self-discovery is like the Silk Road, a meticulous network of interconnected routes. Along these routes, inventions are born, technologies are constructed, and ideas are generated that lead us closer to our authentic selves and our purpose. It is a journey in which we investigate ourselves without judgment.

This guide is meant to bring clarity to your life. For some, this guide will spark curiosity and eagerness as you may feel like a biology student dissecting a lab animal. For others, it may create discomfort as it will challenge your beliefs and contradict your assumptions.

My hope is that you actively read and participate in this journey through this guide. As you read this book, I hope that the crooked paths in your life become straighter and that you walk away with greater awareness, deeper love, and a more profound knowledge of who you really are and the true depth of your potential.

1

JUST BE YOU

●●●●●●●●●●●●●●●●●●●●●●●●●●●●●●●●●●●

Be yourself; everyone else is already taken.
—Oscar Wilde

EMBRACE WHO YOU ARE. EMBRACE YOUR DIFFERENCES—YOUR flaws and quirks—because you're enough all by yourself.

There is so much beauty in witnessing living beings be what they were born to be. Grass is meant to be green—it's meant to grow, it's meant to thrive. Dirt is meant to be brown and dusty or muddy. Grass doesn't try to be dirt any more than dirt tries to be grass. Although they are interdependent and understand their need for each other, they embrace their individuality and are what they were created to be.

Similarly, birds are meant to spread their wings and fly. Cats are meant to meow. A bird doesn't try to meow any more than a cat tries to fly. They, too, are interdependent.

You were created to be you, full of life and authenticity. We each are created to be our individual selves so that we create the perfect balance of color, contrast, and texture to the canvas of life.

You are enough. You have enough vision. You have enough talent and skill. You have enough inner and outer beauty. Embracing your true self is the highest expression of self-love and self-worth. You are worthy to be yourself. You are worthy to just be you.

Reflection

What unique characteristics do you bring to the canvas of life?

Do you find yourself wanting to be someone else?

What is the difference between admiring someone and wanting to be them?

Take Action

In three sentences, summarize what makes you *you*.

What do you do well without trying?

How do people respond to you in your uniqueness?

2

WALK IT OUT

●●●●●●●●●●●●●●●●●●●●●●●●●●●●●●●●●

> *Purpose should speak through your life*
> *well before your lips utter a word.*
> —*Shannon Jones*

EXALTING GOD ON BENDED KNEES WITH LIFTED HANDS IS A GOOD praise. But walking a life of praise by fulfilling your purpose is an even greater praise. Others should witness your purpose without you ever telling them what it is.

Actions speak louder than words. When you walk a life of purpose, you show gratitude for the gift of life and to the giver of life. Living your purpose creates alignment with your mind, body, and soul. This is what brings true happiness.

We each have a purpose to fulfill. All are great in their own special ways.

You don't need to run. You just need to walk. When we walk, we have a greater sense of awareness. We appreciate the journey because we fully participate in learning life's lessons. Life is not a race to be rushed but a walk to be experienced, shared, and enjoyed.

Reflection

Do you know your purpose?

Can people see your purpose without you ever telling them?

Take Action

Ask three people who know you well what they think you do well. Ask them to recall a time when you were passionate about a subject or thing. This passion may have presented itself as frustration or perfectionism. For example, if seeing errors in a document or letter caused you frustration, you could be talented in proofreading or editing. Seek to discover your talents and commit to using your talents daily.

3

A DREAM OR A NIGHTMARE
• •

True success is not measured by you succeeding,
but how you help those who have not succeeded.
—Shannon Jones

THE AMERICAN DREAM DEPICTS A LIFE WITH PERFECT SCENERY.
There are rolling hills and mountains overlooking the Pacific
Coast. There are big houses, fancy cars, elaborate parties, and
world-class catered food. In the background, you hear laughter and
the clinking of wine glasses as people set off cheers while drinking
exquisite cocktails. Instead, the dream is really an infestation of
sorrow hidden behind makeup, smiles, and maxed-out credit cards.

We have been led to believe that riches, fame, and fortune bring
happiness. If that were true, America would make the list of the
top ten happiest countries in the world. Some of the happiest
places to live have little in terms of outward possessions; instead,
they have inward abundance.

Don't let societal ideologies define your dreams of a few name-
brand symbols of fine linens and cars.

Choose to redefine your dreams.

Choose to fight against the current.

Choose to live your best life and help others do the same.

You don't have to accept the nightmare. You can reject the thoughts and opinions of others, to redefine your own dreams.

Reflection

Have you bought into the dogma of success?

Are you living your self-defined dreams, or have you let societal ideologies dictate your dreams?

Are you happy, or are you fappy (faking happiness)?

Are you using worldly possessions or material goods to numb the pain?

Take Action

Write a page on how you use worldly possessions or material goods to define who you are. Read it aloud.

Now, rewrite your story. Describe how you want to experience life on a deeper level to bring true success, happiness, and fulfillment.

Underline the differences in the two stories.

Now, create three action steps to implement true success outlined in your second story.

4

DARKNESS HAS NO POWER
● ●

Look at how a single candle can both
defy and define the darkness.
—*Unknown*

DARKNESS IS DEFINED AS THE TOTAL ABSENCE OF LIGHT.
Therefore, darkness is defined by light and has no identity in and
of itself.
Darkness and light are not equal opposites.
Darkness can't be measured; it can't be quantified or produced.
It is simply what happens when light leaves the room.

You are light.
You have the power to drive out darkness.
You have the power to illuminate all things.

If you are in a dark place emotionally, flip the switch.
For some, light may take the form of prayer or meditation.
For others, it may be phoning a friend or letting go of a toxic relationship.
Whatever it is, remember that darkness has no power. It is simply
the absence of light.

Reflection

Are you currently in a dark place? If yes, what is causing the darkness?

Do you know when to seek help?

Identify two or three friends to share your feelings of unhappiness. Having a support group is essential to overcome dark seasons in your life.

Take Action

Identify one area of darkness in your life.

Now, list two ways you will keep the candle burning. For example, you might seek professional assistance or call a friend.

5

INTUITION

••••••••••••••••••••••••••••••••••

> *How do geese know when to fly to the sun? Who tells*
> *them the seasons? How do we, humans, know when*
> *it is time to move on? How do we know when to go?*
> *As with the migrant birds, so surely with us, there is*
> *a voice within, if only we would listen to it, that tells*
> *us so certainly when to go forth into the unknown.*
> *—Elizabeth Kubler-Ross*

INTUITION IS THE ABILITY TO ACQUIRE KNOWLEDGE WITHOUT proof, evidence, or conscious reasoning, or without understanding how the knowledge was acquired.

The word comes from the Latin word *intueri*, which roughly translated means "to look inside" or "to contemplate."

Intuition is trusting your gut and listening to your inner voice. It's about listening to your inner guide rather than your intellect.

If you want to optimize intuition, you must quiet the mind. Some may quiet the mind through meditation, while others may connect with nature, such as through a nature hike.

Intuition is to humans as instinct is to animals. We each have the natural ability to instinctively know the unknowable and discern which paths to take and what friends to make that draw out our hidden and highest potential. It is one of the greatest gifts given to humankind.

If you honor intuition, pay attention to it. It will show up and be your private internal escort, leading you to natural wonders and warning you of natural disasters.

If you want to know your greatest calling, listen intuitively to what's calling you.

Reflection

When was the last time you listened to your intuition?

Are you aware of its presence when it shows up?

When was the last time you made a decision based on your intuition?

Take Action

Today, spend thirty minutes of quiet time alone. Break up the quiet time into three ten-minute increments. Listen to your breath and clear your thoughts. One of the best ways to enhance your intuition is to clear your thoughts and limit your thinking.

Keep a journal of when you get a gut feeling. Describe how it feels. Does it feel like your intuition or your intellect?

6

SHHH ...

••••••••••••••••••••••••••••••••

> *Listen to silence. It has so much to say.*
> —*Rumi*

SHHH ... IT'S TOO NOISY. I CAN'T THINK. I DON'T KNOW WHO I AM anymore.

Find a quiet place to quiet the mind. When the mind is still, you hear from *you*. A still mind enhances creativity. A still mind reduces stress. A still mind provides clarity of thought.

Be still. If you don't, the noise pollution will cause stress, tension, and anxiety. Noise is defined as a sound—one that is loud or unpleasant or that causes disturbances. Disturbance is defined as an interruption of a settled and peaceful condition. We are under constant attack from daily pressures, expectations, and busyness that we live in a constant state of mental disturbance.

If you don't value your time and what you allow to consume it, you will be consumed. You will lose yourself.

To foster consistency, try to schedule time throughout the day to be still and quiet your mind.

Reflection

What noises are you hearing?

Have you lost yourself due to the noise?

How do you quiet the noise?

Take Action

Designate a quiet place twice a day for meditation. Inhale each breath until it feels like your abdomen will touch your back. Exhale the breath slowly.

Then, follow your breath for the next fifteen minutes.

Silence your phone and give your Internet a rest for one hour. Do this every day.

7

PROBLEM VS. SOLUTION

••••••••••••••••••••••••••••••

*The problem creates the need; the solution fulfills
it. You cannot have one without the other.*
—*Shannon Jones*

WHAT IF YOU SAW EVERY PROBLEM AS AN OPPORTUNITY? WHAT IF
you trusted your own ability to find solutions to your problems?

If you saw your illness as a cure, you just might be healed.
If you saw your job as a vocation, you just might love going to work.

If you saw fear as safety, you just might find peace.
If you saw your limitations as strengths, you just might discover
your calling.

Your problems are opportunities to build skills, create solutions,
and develop confidence. When we solve problems, we grow and
surprisingly stumble on our purpose.

Most of all, one of the greatest gifts that our problems give us
is to help others solve theirs. Through this experience, we learn

that our problem had nothing to do with us but had everything to do with the person we were meant to help. We act as vehicles transporting the solution.

Reflection

How do you see your circumstances? Is your cup half empty or half full?

What is your problem telling you?

What life lessons are you learning from your problem?

Take Action

On a piece of paper, identify at least one growth opportunity that exists within your problem. For example, how is your problem helping you build character and grit?

List how you will leverage this growth opportunity this week.

Write a letter to yourself as if the problem is well behind you. Write about how you plan to help someone else going through the same or a similar problem. Share what steps you took to overcome the obstacle and leverage the obstacle as a growth opportunity.

8

SYNCHRONICITY
• •

> *Synchronicity is a symbiotic agreement that is*
> *spoken in the spirit before manifested on Earth.*
> —*Shannon Jones*

NOTHING JUST HAPPENS. THERE IS A REASON FOR EVERYTHING, and everything has a reason.

Synchronicity is a phenomenon in which things fall in place that simply cannot be reasoned. It's like an imaginary person pulling the puppet strings to make things happen. It's like a mysterious creature without a single origin; it just shows up and sprinkles fairy dust, creating magical connections.

Synchronicity provides clues to guide our paths. It knows you. It nudges you because it wants to give you something. It desires your attention.

If you ignore it, you forfeit your greatest opportunities that lead you to your dreams and destiny.

If you don't pay attention, it will show up less and less. If you take it for granted, it will stop giving.

It you fail to decipher its meaning, the mystery will never be revealed. But if you watch and listen carefully, you will welcome the greatest manifestation of miracles that life has to offer.

Reflection

What coincidences have you ignored in the past month?
Do you listen intently to synchronicity?

Take Action

Think back to a time when extraordinary events occurred. What happened? What was the meaning?

List one thing that you will do to help you gain greater awareness of coincidences in your life.

9

CHILL OUT

• •

It's really important to have balance, spend
some time in nature, go to a few parties,
enjoy my friends, and really chill out.
—Joakim Noah

WE LIVE IN A WORLD FULL OF STRESS, EXPECTATIONS, AND responsibilities. We are in such a rush that it can be hard to catch a breath. As a result, we are exhausted. We are fearful. We are frustrated. We are restless. We are depleted.

Under these conditions, we must be intentional in replenishing our mind, body, and soul. We must let our hair down and enjoy nature and friends. We must find time to just chill out.

When we find time to chill out, we offset exhaustion for energy; fear for fearlessness; frustration for satisfaction; restlessness for peace; depletion for replenishment. A healthy life is dependent on this balance.

Reflection

Do you have a healthy balance of enjoyable activities to offset stress?

Is there an opportunity to rid some stressors in your life?

Take Action

List three things that have you feeling exhausted, fearful, frustrated, and/or restless.

List at least one activity that you enjoy doing (e.g., eating out with friends, dancing, playing sports, etc.). Beside the activity, express why you enjoy this activity.

Now, commit to how often you will engage in each activity per month.

10

WHAT KIND OF DRIVER ARE YOU?
• •

You may be the driver, but what's driving you?
—Shannon Jones

ONE OF THE BEST WAYS TO DETERMINE OUR LEVEL OF STRESS IS TO monitor our attitude while driving. Driving is a subconscious activity. We do it without thought or awareness. The subconscious mind showcases our default programming when responding to events, activities, and stressors.

Your driving behavior speaks directly to parts of your attitude. Are you an aggressive driver? Are you a cautious driver? Are you a rushed driver? Are you a kind driver?

If you pay close attention, many of these same behaviors show up when we respond to other circumstances and people in our life. Many of these responses are subconscious reactions to daily activities and stressful events.

Reflection

Contemplate what kind of driver you are most of the time.

What subconscious attitudes or behaviors serve as your default?

Take Action

The next time you are driving, monitor your attitude and behavior.

Create awareness by correlating how your driving behavior shows up in other areas of your life, such as how you treat others and respond to events.

Lastly, take steps to reprogram your subconscious mind, such as:

1. Being fully present and aware.
2. Using powerful words and affirmations.
3. Controlling negative thoughts and replacing them with positive ones.
4. Creating intentions that support well-being.

11

SAVOR LIFE

• •

Life tastes good, if you season it right.
—Shannon Jones

BREATHE.
Slow down.
How does coffee smell?
What flavors do you taste in your three-cheese herb omelet?
Do you taste the thyme and roasted fennel?

Life is meant to be savored and enjoyed.

If not:
Chew a little longer.
Sip a little slower.
Smell a little deeper.
Hug a little tighter.
Laugh a little louder.
Listen a little harder.
Give a little more.
Aim a little higher.

Love a little broader.
Smile a little wider.
Dig a little deeper.
Seek a little humor.
Grow a little wiser.
Work a little smarter.
Play a little rougher.
Live a little happier.
Dream a little bigger.

Appreciate a lot more.

Reflection

When was the last time you stopped to notice a flower? What vivid colors did you notice? How did it smell?

Take Action

Savor something today. For example, before you drink your morning beverage, inhale, and smell the aroma.

When you consume a meal today, try to taste and distinguish each ingredient. Appreciate the tastes and textures. Slowing down will enhance the experience and create mindfulness and gratitude.

12

IMAGINE THIS

● ●

> *If the mind has the capacity to see it and the*
> *heart has the capacity to receive it, then the*
> *Almighty has the capability to release it.*
> —*Shannon Jones*

IMAGINE THAT THERE ARE NO LIMITATIONS.

You are free to go where you wish.
Money is plentiful.
Resources are abundant.
People are waiting to assist you.
Nothing is missing, nothing is lacking.
You have vision.
You have provision.
You have the fortitude.
Possibilities are endless.
There are no limitations, only opportunities.
Only solutions exist.

Now that you have everything you need to make your life work,
all your life needs now is *you*.

Reflection

Could you be your only limitation?

What have you always wanted to do or become?

Are you living your highest calling?

Take Action

Fold a piece of paper in half. Label one side "What I have" and the other "What I need." Make a list of what you have and what you need. In making your list, make sure that what you have includes both internal and external resources. For example, if you need help building a website, ask yourself who could assist, such as a friend or colleague. These are all external helpers that should be included as existing resources.

The purpose of this exercise is to help you see that you have more than what you don't have. This exercise will also help you develop a sense of community by seeking assistance from others. We are all interconnected. The universe already knows what you need, which is why it has placed specific people around you to help you meet your needs, just as you are there to help others' meet their needs. Open your eyes and ears, and seek.

13

MOONSHINE

••••••••••••••••••••••••••••••••••

The moon provides light in the midst of darkness;
that external light creates internal illumination.
—*Shannon Jones*

I DIDN'T GET INTOXICATED BY AN ILLICIT SUBSTANCE. INSTEAD, I became intoxicated by the moon shining so brightly in my bathroom window.

All lights were off, as I laid in my bathtub full of steamy hot, bubbly water. I felt as if I was being watched. I was—by the moon. It wanted my attention. It wanted to talk. I didn't. I twisted the blinds to force an even greater closure as if to say, "Goodnight and leave me alone." It didn't listen. It continued to shine boldly into my bathroom.

I surrendered. I looked into its eyes. We had the loveliest conversation. So much so, that I became intoxicated by its words. It said nothing. Its presence said everything. Its presence said I am your shining light, and I will guide you through what appears to be a dark place. It said that darkness has no power. I smiled and it smiled back.

Reflection

Is there a shining light in your life that you haven't noticed that could assist you on this journey of life?

Are you open to listening to what it has to say?

Take Action

What's trying to get your attention? Don't ignore it. It has a message for you.

This week, be sensitive to life's subtle nudges from nature, life, or people. It has a voice if you will listen. Journal what you discover.

14

LOSE TO WIN

• •

I am not bound to win; I am bound to be
true. I am not bound to succeed, but I am
bound to live up to the light I have.
—*Abraham Lincoln*

SOMETIMES YOU MUST CHOOSE TO SURRENDER AND LET GO. YOU can't win them all. Losing never feels good. Neither does winning.

After all, you have won nearly all your life, right? I mean, you did everything in the right order—a college graduate, no babies out of wedlock, career, marriage, a new home, then kids.

You later learned that the college degree didn't get you the job of your dreams. The career is a money-making prison. The marriage is lifeless. The house is falling apart. You are so busy with kid stuff that you have no real time for your kids.

How does winning feel? You see, winning doesn't feel good either.

But are you really winning?

Sometimes losing means you choose not to play the game any longer. It means you don't care about what others think. It means you no longer care about the fake success, and you are ready to expose the fake love. It means you choose to be your authentic self, even if your outward imagery is failure.

Sometimes losing means finding yourself. Sometimes losing is winning.

Reflection

Do you care what people think of you or the life you've chosen to live?

What does authenticity look like for you?

Take Action

Take a sheet of paper, fold it in half vertically, and then fold it in half horizontally to create four quadrants.

On the top left side of the page, write down areas where you are winning in life. On the top right side of the page, write down ways you are losing in life.

Next, on the bottom left side of the page, write why and how you are winning. For example, are you winning because you are living your life by your own standards?

What are some strategies you are using to win? On the bottom right side of the page, write why you are losing.

Next, compare the winning lists top to bottom and see how you can create wins from the losing list.

The purpose of this exercise is to develop an awareness for the strategies you are using that have created the wins so that you can replicate them in other areas of your life.

15

*YOU*NIQUE

• •

> *You are so unique, that your uniqueness is so*
> *complex that your gene expression is easily*
> *distinguished from any other species.*
> —*Shannon Jones*

WHEN YOU WAKE UP EVERY MORNING, YOU SHOULD THANK GOD for two things. First, thank God for God and secondly, thank God for *you* because you're the second-best miracle ever created.

You are gifted, talented, and experienced. Put all these together and you have the ability to perform your own miracles. You have a culmination of gifts, talents, and experiences that no one else has in the world.

There is only one *you*. There is no one else who can do the things that you do in the way you do them. No one can bring it quite like you bring it! You are unique. You can't be replicated. Your gene expression is different. Your neurochemistry is different. Your temperament is different; your voice, fingers, and thought patterns are different. You are distinct.

Now that you have thanked God for *you*, thank *you* for *you* because you are the second-best miracle given to the world. Now, go and create your own miracles.

Reflection

Are you grateful for you?
Do you embrace your uniqueness?

Take Action

Create a list of your unique characteristics that set you apart. In creating this list, identify how best to leverage these differences to showcase its beauty and strength. I recall how beauty has changed over the past several years in the fashion and modeling industries. We now see models who have distinct traits such as freckles, unibrows, or tooth gaps. At one time, these traits were considered weaknesses. Never let your uniqueness be an embarrassment; instead, let it serve as a strength.

16

THE FIVE A'S OF HUMAN LANGUAGE

••••••••••••••••••••••••••••••••••

Love is a language that apprehends pain and suffering.
—Shannon Jones

THE FIVE A'S ARE: ATTENTION, APPRECIATION, ACCEPTANCE, AFFECTION, and ALLOWANCE. The five A's are the foundation of all friendships and relationships. Similarly, the letter "A" is the foundation of the English alphabet. Without the letter A, the letters B through Z wouldn't exist.

When you give someone your *attention*, you act in a state of complete awareness—fully conscious and alert in the present moment.

When you *appreciate* someone, you acknowledge the value they bring to your life and the world.

When you *accept* someone, you remove all judgment and detach from an outcome of what you envision or hope them to be. You accept them for who they are, not who they could or will be or who you want them to be.

When you show *affection* to someone, you express kindness and form an emotional bond.

When you express *allowance* to someone, you give them the freedom to explore and just be.

There are five A's. The number five represents balance, as seen in the human body—five fingers and toes, and the five senses (sight, hearing, taste, smell, and touch).

The best way to implement the five A's is to just simply love. If we learn to truly love, the five A's are a guarantee—an automatic. It's a buy one, get five free. And all you have to do is love me.

Reflection

Are you receiving each of the five A's in your relationships?

Are you giving each of the five A's in your relationships?

Take Action

Take an assessment of your most significant relationships. Do they contain all the five A's? If not, which of the five A's are missing?

How can you incorporate the five A's to build stronger relationships both on the giving and receiving ends?

17

I CHOOSE

• •

The power of the mind can start a fire and
command rain from the sky to consume it.
—*Shannon Jones*

TODAY IS AN AWESOME AND AMAZING DAY. IT'S NOT BECAUSE I necessarily feel awesome and amazing, but because I choose to make a conscious choice that today is going to be a good day.

I choose to look on the brighter side of life's circumstances because darkness is so tangible. Darkness can be touched without ever reaching for it. It can be seen without ever looking for it. It can be smelled without ever inhaling it. Sometimes darkness comes so that light can be appreciated.

Darkness has no place because I give it no power. I see the lack, the evil, and sadness, but I choose not to stare at it. It's not that I'm naïve, deceived, or live in a world of make-believe. Instead, I choose to cleave to things that build and not destroy; things that compliment and not insult; things that unite and not divide; things of hope and not despair.

I choose to be a doer; a server; an encourager; a motivator. I choose to be light; to live and give with all my might. Even if my doing is done at night, out of sight from all to see, I still serve just because it's right.

I choose to spread positive words and do good deeds. My gift to the world is to plant and water seeds of hope and fulfill others' needs.

Reflection

Are you mostly optimistic or pessimistic?

How can you facilitate optimism in your life without ignoring reality?

Take Action

List one thing that you can do to change your mindset to be more optimistic.

List three things that went well today.

What caused them to go well?

18

THANK YOU

• •

*Gratitude is recognizing that someone shared a piece
of themselves with you, no matter how large or small.*
—*Shannon Jones*

THANK YOU FOR LOVING ME.
Thank you for being my friend.
Thank you for preparing my meal.
Thank you for safety.
Thank you for being kind.
Thank you for valuing me.
Thank you for your sincere apology.
Thank you for forgiveness.
Thank you for the reward and recognition.
Thank you for the compliment.
Thank you for the constructive feedback.
Thank you for listening compassionately.
Thank you for protecting my feelings.
Thank you for your support.
Thank you for the mentorship.
Thank you for opening the door.

Thank you for the borrowed money.
Thank you for the insights.
Thank you for celebrating me.
Thank you for not judging me
Thank you for your honesty and integrity.
Thank you for being loyal and trustworthy.
Thank you for being curious about me.
Thank you for being respectful and polite.
Thank you for your patience and diplomacy.
Thank you for your altruism.
Thank you for your positive perspective.
Thank you for serving me.
Thank you for your keen emotional intelligence.
Thank you for your wisdom and self-mastery.
Thank you for making my life easier.
Thank you for making me better.
Thank you for accepting me just as I am.
Thank you for letting me know that I matter.
Thank you for ensuring that your actions align with your words.
Thank you, thank you, thank you!

Reflection

When was the last time you told someone *thank you*?

Take Action

From the *thank you* acknowledgements above, circle at least five acknowledgments that you have personally experienced and benefited from others.

Now, write names beside the circled acknowledgments of those you want to thank.

Next, write thank-you note to the people on your list. The thank-you notes should express your gratitude for their generosity.

Lastly, deliver the thank-you notes.

19

EXTREME SPORTS

....

I choose to live hard because living soft
leaves no footprints in the sand.
—Shannon Jones

EXTREME SPORTS ARE RECREATIONAL ACTIVITIES THAT INVOLVE A high degree of risk. These activities often involve speed and a high level of physical exertion.

Life is an extreme sport.

Life is about working hard. Work until you obtain the results you want.

Life is about playing hard. Play until you create your own games and break every rule.

Life is about loving hard. Love until your heart becomes soft.

Life is about laughing hard. Laugh until you cry.

Life is about being. Being what you want to see. It's about becoming who you want to be.

Life is an extreme sport. It is about engaging in recreational and social activities, spending quality time with friends and loved ones, and enjoying your favorite pastimes.

Life is an extreme sport. In order to live life well, you must take a high degree of risks. If you play it safe, you live recklessly as you gamble the only life you have.

Extreme sports are about climbing the highest mountain. They're about speed and agility.

Extreme sports are about giving life your all, until physical and mental exhaustion sets in from pursuing the life you want. Only then will you know that you are giving life all you've got.

Reflection

Are you present in your life?

Are you living your life or are you on autopilot?

Take Action

For an entire week, observe your life. Observe what you do throughout the day on weekdays and weekends, and at work and home.

Are you going through the motions?

Are you doing things in a mediocre manner versus putting forth your full effort?

Make a list of the following:

1. Current projects or goals that you are actively pursuing that excite you? These projects could be professional or personal goals.
2. Meaningful conversations you had with a friend, coworker, or family member who inspired you to live your greatest life.

Create goals with time frames to facilitate accountability. The purpose of this activity is to create measurable changes in your life that you can reflect upon and be proud.

20

LOST AND FOUND
••••••••••••••••••••••••••••••••••••

We may be temporarily separated from the
tracks, but the tracks are never far away.
—Shannon Jones

HAVE YOU EVER WANDERED SLOWLY THROUGH THE WOODS
without following any directions or time schedules? Have you
ever focused on getting lost in "just being," until you became
walking meditation? Inhaling and exhaling slowly, listening to
every breath. Tuning out all voices and noises and setting an
intention to simply just get lost.

This process can be therapeutic because it breaks up the schedule
and routine of life. We wake up at the same time, start work at the
same time, work on the same or similar tasks, day in and day out.
Are we prisoners of life? If so, we must slowly saw-off the prison
bars from our minds by adding more spontaneity, taking more
risks, switching up our daily routines, and working on projects
that inspire us. As we do this, we realize that we were never lost,
but only in search of ourselves.

Reflection

Do you feel lost?

Do you feel both lost and found? For example, you may have clear direction in one aspect of your life but have no direction in another aspect of your life.

Take Action

We will not always have answers to life's questions. We have to trust life; trust that if we do our part, that it will do its part. Take a mindful walk outdoors and ponder the questions for which you are seeking answers. As you trust life through the uncertainty, you'll discover that the human experience is about being both lost and found.

21

SMILES

• •

Smiles spread kindness that transcends
language differences, mental intelligence,
and physical disabilities. It is a universal
language that everyone can understand.
—*Shannon Jones*

SMILES ARE SPONTANEOUS ACTS OF KINDNESS. THEY ARE SILENT acts of gratitude. They exude happiness and universal oneness. The stranger who shares one, understands that we are all connected without ever knowing each other. The receiver feels that they are seen for who they are.

Smiles are contagious. They are reciprocal gestures. An authentic smile is an expression of love and kindness. A smile is priceless. It warms the heart and soul.

It's a universal language that everyone understands and speaks. A smile fully embodies the law of attraction. A smile can be heard and felt over the phone through energy exchange.

A smile can come through your eyes and through your entire being. Your body language can serve as a smile. A smile is a state of mind. It is a way of being.

Reflection

When was the last time you smiled at someone?

When was the last time you made someone smile?

Take Action

A smile can be seen, heard, and felt. Are you using your five senses to smile? In this new world of face masks, you can see and sense a smile without ever seeing a person's mouth. You can see a smile in a person's eyes and body language.

Create an intention to use your entire being to serve as a smile to lift someone's spirits and show them they matter.

Today, smile at five people using your entire being.

22

JUICE YOUR LIFE
•••••••••••••••••••••••••••••••••••

I plan to squeeze every ounce of talent from my
life so that nothing is left, not even the rind.
—Shannon Jones

FRESHLY SQUEEZED JUICE TASTE NOTHING LIKE STORE-BOUGHT. IT
has no preservatives or additives. It has only one ingredient: juice
from raw fruits and vegetables. It tastes so good that you try your
hardest to squeeze out every ounce of natural sweetness. When
you finally drink it, it is worth the strained muscles and fatigued
hands.

Freshly squeezed juice is like *you*. It has only one ingredient. It is
all-natural and full of goodness.

The juicing process is intentional. The juicer's purpose is to
enforce pressure to extract powerful nutrients, such as vitamins and
minerals, from the vessel. The juicing process involves grinding,
twisting, and squeezing to release goodness and wholesomeness.
A great juicer will then take the leftovers (rind, scraps, and skin)
and make good use of them. Nothing goes to waste.

A life that has been thoroughly juiced resembles both a raisin and a pitcher of juice. With the raisin, the juice has been removed from the grape which is indicative of pulling out and using all of your talents, skills and gifts. The pitcher of juice is indicative of you using the juice from the grape that produced the raisin to assist mankind. Once this life has been thoroughly juiced, the goal is to empty the pitcher by filling up all the cups that surround it—pouring your talents, gifts, and abilities into others.

Reflection

What does your life resemble?

Are you squeezing every ounce of juice from your life?

Are you leaving juice in the vessel to be discarded?

Take Action

Picture your life as a piece of fruit or a vegetable. Would it be completely unjuiced, a little juiced, or completely juiced? What does a completely juiced life—where you are living your highest potential—look like for you? For example, does it look like you becoming a great teacher to pour hope into students? Start defining what a *juiced life* resembles in your life. While you ponder these questions, physically juice an orange for inspiration. As you are grinding and twisting the orange, think about the gifts and talents that need to pour out of you and into someone else. Think about gifts that lie dormant that deserve to come out. Your goal should be to squeeze a little juice each day until there's nothing left. Starting today, commit to using your talents to serve others.

23

DON'T MISS YOUR SEASON

. . . .

> *Since seasons are time-sensitive, one must be*
> *hypersensitive to manifest their dreams.*
> —*Shannon Jones*

EVERYTHING HAS A SEASON. THERE IS A TIME TO PLANT AND A TIME to harvest. There is a time to move and a time to be still. There is a time for peace and a time for war. There is a time to spend and a time to save.

When you are operating in your season, supernatural forces intercede on your behalf, creating wins just waiting to be manifested on earth. When you operate in your season, everything works together to reveal your calling.

It is possible to do the right thing at the wrong time. It is possible to miss your season. There is a period when your season is optimized. You wouldn't expect a man to wait until he's eighty years old to begin a career in major league baseball, or a woman to become a new mom at the age of eighty. An investor doesn't invest when there is no chance for a return, no more than a farmer plants vegetables to be harvested the next day.

There is a season in which you operate at your best, in which your gifts are optimized. There is a season in which you have the stamina and grace to function at your highest. There is a season in which the orchestra is on one accord, rendering a standing ovation. Don't miss your season.

Reflection

Are you optimizing this season in your life?

Take Action

Think about what you should be doing in this season.

Write down a three-month plan, month to month.

Next, create a six-month plan. The plan should be specific and capture measurable goals and objectives month to month to help you stay on task. For example, if you want to switch careers, what career are you specifically seeking?

What skills and talents do you possess to fully support and optimize this switch? Next, create a plan to transition to this new career using SMART (Specific, Measurable, Action, Results, Timeline) goals.

24

RAIN AND TEARS

••••••••••••••••••••••••••••••••••••

> *Rain and tears are so fluid that they stretch across*
> *every corner and seep into every crevice to penetrate*
> *and permeate every surface. When they reach*
> *their destination, they wash, clear, and heal.*
> —*Shannon Jones*

RAIN CLEANS AND RINSES. TEARS WASH AND CLEAR. WATER COMES from a pure source, an intentional place. It comes from a high place beyond your problems and pain. Your tears form many times because of problems and pain, and yet they have the same healing properties as rain. Both flow and move to create healing.

When you empty out your tears, you release endorphins that act as pain relievers to shift the mood of your brain. When it rains, the rain cleans, washes, and clears. When it rains, the sky is cloudy. The sun doesn't shine. When we cry, we usually experience pain. But something magical happens once the rains stops— once the tears dry up. The sun comes out ever so bright, bright as the smile on a baby's face. Flowers start to bloom just as you start to heal.

You see, rain is necessary for growth just as tears are necessary for healing. Rain falls, creating puddles; tears flow after the creation of sorrow, but tomorrow, the rainbow will create a bridge by which you can walk over the puddle and persevere through the sorrow.

Reflection

Have you experienced a lot of pain and sorrow throughout your life?

Contemplate how you have grown from pain and sorrow.

Take Action

Think about how you can use your pain and sorrow to heal and to help someone in need. Share your story with at least one person this week to encourage them that a better tomorrow will come. Part of your healing process is to help someone else heal. Remember that awareness of the pain brings wisdom. Your wisdom is meant to be shared with others.

25

DEAR TEACHER

•••••••••••••••••••••••••••••••••••••

I'm a student of life, and the universe is my classroom.
—Shannon Jones

THANK YOU FOR COMING INTO MY LIFE AND PRESENTING CLASSROOM
lessons. Although, I completed grade school, undergrad, and post-
grad, I am still in this classroom. I am tired of taking notes; I am
tired of taking tests. No more homework, group discussions, or
projects, please. I have walked across every stage, worn many caps
and gowns, and yet I am still in this classroom. This classroom
is not to test my knowledge in chemistry, anatomy, biology,
or trigonometry. It's here to test my knowledge in, kindness,
servitude, charity, generosity, and integrity.

You have come into my life to give me life lessons. I may not always
enjoy meet-the-teacher night, because I'm always meeting new
teachers. Whether it be a new friend, a stranger on an airplane,
or an acquaintance. Sometimes, I don't meet them; instead, I read
about them. I see them on TV. Sometimes, they are animals.

Dear teacher, you will use anything to get my attention, to guide me, steer me, and chastise me—to teach me valuable lessons.

Dear teacher, you are testing my knowledge, understanding, and application in this classroom called life. You want to know if I am learning from these life lessons and be assured that your efforts are not in vain. You want to know if I am evolving and thriving, pursuing life and my purpose. You want me to review my notes, apply them to the test, and participate in group discussions to assist mankind. You want me to actively participate in my life and know that our paths have crossed for a specific reason.

Dear teacher, although you are the teacher, I am also teaching you.

Reflection

Are you listening to the lessons that life teach you daily?
What lesson did it teach today?
How will you apply this lesson to your life?

Take Action

This week, practice listening to the lessons that life offers you. Keep a pen and pad with you to jot down these lessons. You may receive nudges throughout the day that provide you "aha" moments. These nudges could be lessons on staying calm or taming your ego. Whichever vehicle comes to teach a life lesson, be open to the lesson. This exercise will require you to increase your awareness by listening consciously. After you have learned and applied the lesson, it is time to teach the lesson.

26

I DESERVE TO BE KNOWN.
I DESERVE FRIENDSHIP.
••••••••••••••••••••••••••••••••••••

Curiosity is the greatest expression of friendship.
—Shannon Jones

HOW IS IT THAT YOU'VE KNOWN ME NEARLY HALF OF MY LIFE AND still don't know me? If I asked you to tell me only one of my passions, you could only conjure up my disinterests. If I asked you to recall only one book I've read, you wouldn't know. If I asked you to share one of my many strengths, you would only come up with weaknesses.

How is it that I am in your presence routinely, and you not know me? How is it that I make you tick, and you don't know what ticks me off? How is it that I fuel you daily, and you don't know what fuels me? A stranger could answer most of these questions after a fifteen-minute conversation.

I just want to be known by you. While, I may never be known by you, the greatest lesson is that I deserve to know myself. I deserve my own friendship. Now, I know that you were never curious about knowing me because I was never curious about knowing myself.

I deserve to be known by me. I deserve my own friendship.

Reflection

Do you know yourself?

Do you spend time getting to know yourself as you evolve and change?

Take Action

Today, commit to learning yourself more deeply.

Do you know why you do what you do?

Do you know why you react to certain situations as you do?

Seek meaning in the "why" to reveal the meaning or lesson to help move you forward. This can provide major insights toward discovering your purpose and calling, or areas that need healing.

Also, assess patterns that show up in your life. Patterns are useful in making predictions. If there are patterns that you don't like, you have the power to change them and create new ones.

27

ATTENTION = FOCUS = ENERGY

....

What gets your attention, commands your
focus and demands your energy.
—*Shannon Jones*

WHAT HAS YOUR ATTENTION, HAS YOUR FOCUS; AND WHAT HAS YOUR focus, has your energy. Our attention should be spent on reaching our highest potential. Our focus should support our purpose, goals, and ambitions. Our energy is so precious that only deserving efforts that strengthen and support our well-being should claim it.

What has your energy, has your time. Time can be spent on worrying, stressing, or being satisfied. It can show up as depletion, apathy, or excitement.

When our attention is on a situation that is out of our control, our focus may be spent on controlling what can't be controlled. In turn, our energy may show up as fear and frustration.

If our attention is on surrendering to a situation and releasing what we can't control, our focus will be spent on embracing the unknown, which yields the energies of peace and hope.

We decide what gets our attention, focus, and energy. Choose what will get your energy. What has your energy, has your time.

To assess our attention, focus, and energy, disconnect to reconnect. Say no to say yes. Shut down to turn on. Lose yourself in silence to find yourself out loud.

Reflection

What has your attention and focus?

What does the energy of your attention and focus look like?

Take Action

This week, keep a journal of how you spend your time and energy. Try to capture all your daily activities.

List important activities and responsibilities as well as time zappers.

Next, list the amount of time you devote to each activity.

Then, circle your time zappers.

Now, create a plan for how you will limit time zappers, by how much, and how you will replace them with positive energy-fueling activities.

Time zappers include time spent on social media, watching TV, or gossiping with a friend or colleague. It could take the form of being in a dead-end relationship. Time zappers have no investment value.

The goal of this activity is to create a greater level of awareness so that your energy is put to good use through mindfulness.

28

STOP, DROP, AND ROLL
• •

Life can be a ferocious fire devouring
everything in sight. The closer you get to the
ground, the more the fire loses its fight.
—Shannon Jones

WE ARE TAUGHT AT AN EARLY AGE THAT FIRE IS DANGEROUS. During school fire drills, we are taught that the minute we see fire or smoke we are to stop, drop, and roll. What are we taught to do when we encounter a problem? Some are taught to phone a friend, while others are taught to fight fire with fire. Few are taught to be still. *Stop* what you're doing. *Drop* to your knees. And *roll* to lie prostrate in prayer.

Why do we share our problems with everyone but God? Why is it that we turn to God as our last resort? God created us and all things, including the universe. He has the manufacturer's handbook. He is the solution. He knows just what we endure. He knows all about the pain and suffering. He wants to reassure us that we can go through things without allowing things to go through us. In order to hear this message, we must stop, drop, and roll. Fire safety instructions are there to protect us in the physical world. These same instructions can serve to protect us emotionally and spiritually. In both instances, the hope is that we safely escape and not be consumed by the fire physically, spiritually, or emotionally.

The next time you encounter a problem, *stop, drop, and roll*.

Reflection

Whom or where do you turn to when trouble hits your life?

If fire has an opponent, what can you use to put it out?

Take Action

Think about a time when you were faced with great difficulty. What did you do? Did you complain and wallow in self-pity, or did you *stop, drop, and roll*?

Looking back at a problem, did it eventually work itself out?

If you were to go through that problem today, what would you do differently?

What strategies could you apply when you are faced with a future difficulty?

Effective strategies include meditation, prayer, and reflecting on why you are facing the difficulty. If your strategy includes phoning a friend, choose a friend who empowers you and inspires you to be a victor in the time of trouble.

29

FORGIVE YOURSELF

*Self-forgiveness is loving yourself
until your self is forgiven.*
—*Shannon Jones*

DO YOU HAVE A PROBLEM WITH FORGIVING YOURSELF? IF YOU LACK forgiveness in your heart, let it go. Unforgiveness is liked pouring salt on a snail which melts away the flesh.

The cure for unforgiveness is love.

How is it possible that poison is also a cure? A venomous snakebite is deadly, but its venom also gives life as it is the antidote to the very condition it caused. Could it be that the very thing that is hurting you, could heal you? How can you turn your pain into love? Your despair into hope? How can you turn your unforgiveness into a message of forgiveness?

The man who was once a criminal, now visits the prison to give hope to criminals.

If you are angry about your decisions in life, help others avoid taking the same path you took.

If you feel like you have wasted time in a dead-end career, switch careers or become a guidance counselor to help others find their career paths.

Many times, it's through our pain that we find our purpose and healing. Only you can deliver this powerful message, as you have lived it. Let your mess become your message. When you allow your mess to become your message, pain exits the body—joy enters the body and love enters the heart.

Reflection

Is it difficult for you to forgive yourself?

Do you find that it's easier to forgive others?

Do you believe that you deserve forgiveness?

Take Action

The first step toward forgiving yourself is to realize that you are not meant to be perfect—no one is. Think about an area in which you struggle to forgive yourself. Write it on a piece of paper.

Next, write answers to the following questions:

1. How can you turn your unforgiveness into a message of hope for others?
2. What did you learn from this painful experience?
3. What steps do you need to take to love yourself?

30

EGOS VS. EAGLES

• •

> *One has to lose their inner ego*
> *to find their outer eagle.*
> —*Shannon Jones*

BOTH EGOS AND EAGLES FLY HIGH. THEY ARE BOTH FLESH-EATING mammals. Both enjoy being on the mountaintop. They are both dominant. One is foul, the other is a kind of fowl.

Egos fly high but will eventually plummet. Eagles fly high and soar as they are carried by the wind.

Egos eat when they are not hungry because they yearn for greed. Eagles eat to survive.

Egos enjoy being on the mountaintop for all to see—to see their grandeur. Eagles visit the mountaintop for safety and protection from predators.

Egos can't see past themselves. Eagles have great vision and foresight.

Reflection

How do you manage your ego?

Are you intentional in showcasing your eagle?

Take Action

We all have egos. The ego is an inflated sense of self. Starting today, perform daily ego checks until the ego is less prominent and the eagle becomes more prominent in your life.

31

DINNER

• •

Food gives life. Food with friends gives abundance.
—*Shannon Jones*

DINNER IS MORE THAN JUST AN AFTERNOON RITUAL TO REFUEL
our fatigued bodies. It's more than a social norm. Dinner is about
sharing and giving to those we like, love, and enjoy. Having
dinner with friends or loved ones yields a net positive value. It
says, "I want to spend this time with you to learn more about you
and to share myself with you." It's about deepening a relationship.
It's about savoring life as we savor our food in that very moment.

Dinner is about gratitude—gratitude for great friendships,
gratitude for sincere conversations, gratitude for laughter and
fellowship. It's about gratitude for safety in sharing our fears,
failures, and vulnerabilities, and never being judged for them.
Dinner is about being grateful for having the means to afford a
ribeye steak dinner with garlic seared mashed potatoes, roasted
asparagus, and julienne heirloom carrots. It's about thanking the
rancher who supplied the cow and the butcher who butchered the

cow. It's about thanking the farmer who grew the vegetables. It's thanking those who prepared the food.

It's about connecting with the soil, nature, and creation. It's about basking in the present. It's about being aware that you have a lot more than what others have in the world.

Dinner is much more than eating a meal. It's a holistic experience and an expression of love. Now, I know why we say grace.

Reflection

When was the last time you had dinner with friends? What did you most enjoy about the camaraderie?

Take Action

The next time you have dinner with friends, be completely present in the moment and fully experience the great friendship, sincere conversation, and meal.

Also, be thankful for the servers by treating them with respect and decency. When you savor your meal, think about the hands that grew it—the hands that picked it, the hands that processed it, the hands that prepared it, and the hands that served it. Say a silent prayer for each of them.

32

YOU ARE NOT WHAT YOU DID

· ·

You are separated from your actions,
when you learn from them.
—Shannon Jones

STEALING DOESN'T MAKE ONE A THIEF. SIMILARLY, TELLING A white lie doesn't make one a liar. Cheating doesn't make one a cheater. Drinking liquor doesn't make one a drunk. Flunking out of school doesn't make one a dummy. Using drugs doesn't make one a drug addict. Being alone doesn't mean one is lonely.

You are not what you did. What you did doesn't define you. You are more than what you did.

Reflection

Think of a time when you disappointed yourself.

Did you learn from that disappointing choice? What did you learn?

Take Action

Accept that you are not perfect; the human experience never is. The human experience involves victories and defeats. Anticipate that you will make poor choices, however, commit to not repeating those same poor choices. If you have hurt others due to your poor choices, seek to make things right.

33

FOOD HALL

● ●

Do at least one thing well, or do nothing at all.
—*Shannon Jones*

A FOOD HALL IS SIMILAR TO THE AMERICAN FOOD COURT, BUT instead of serving fast food, local food artists specialize in serving the best food concoctions and flavor profiles. Chefs create intimacy and mastery of food items. This perfection is achieved by creating limits on the number of food items served to avoid mediocrity. Each chef is at the top of their game. Food halls are full of consistency, mastery, and synergy.

What if you created an internal food hall, where you specialized in doing at least one thing well versus many things okay? Where you drew wholesome people into your life with an appetite for quality. Where you surrounded yourself with like-minded individuals who pushed you to greatness. Where you placed limits on the number of things that got your attention. If you viewed your life as a food hall, you could create some of the world's greatest inventions. You could be one of the world's greatest philanthropists promoting generosity to satisfy the palate of human welfare.

Reflection

What have you nearly perfected?

Have you nearly perfected something that make you proud?

Take Action

List one area or thing in your life that you strive for perfection. For example, are you great at cooking, baking, etc.? Other examples include reading, writing, or editing. Are you good at leading and managing? If you have trouble thinking of an area that you have strived to make perfect, identify one thing that you're good at or can be good at. Everyone is good or can be great at something, so keep searching until you identify at least one thing. Once you have identified one thing, commit today to doing it well.

34

LAUGH UNTIL IT HURTS

·····································

When you laugh until it hurts,
your hurt turns to laughter.
—*Shannon Jones*

WHEN WAS THE LAST TIME YOU LAUGHED UNTIL YOU CRIED? UNTIL you wet your pants. Until your stomach muscles ached. If you can't remember, it's been way too long.

Laughter is therapeutic. It's that goofy friend who says something out of the blue and you burst out laughing because you simply cannot hold it in. All the while, your laughter clears out the mucus in your head and erases all the bad memories you've been fed.

It neutralizes stress, similar to how baking soda neutralizes odors. Baking soda lowers the pH as laughter lowers the ACTH. Laughter improves your mood, similar to how salt stabilizes food. It promotes the feel-good endorphins, similar to morphine. It acts as a pain-reliever without the risk of addiction. It can destroy friction and ease tension. It's one of the easiest ways to get a six-pack, and it shifts the brain like dark chocolate does in a KitKat.

I hope you are convinced that laughter can put a dent in your depression and limit your aggression.

35

TAP OUT

• •

I referee my own life; I decide when
to stay or get out of the ring.
—*Shannon Jones*

I AM IN THIS RING WRESTLING WITH YOU YET ANOTHER DAY. YOU won a round and were crowned. I won two and promised myself that I was completely through. The next day, we are on this same battleground. I am dizzy on this merry-go-round. When I offer my opinion, it gets dismissed. I can't go another round as I am tired and uninspired. I can't stick around as I don't have the energy to rebound. At one point, you had me spellbound. Now we can't find common ground. My emotions are drowning in stress, and the only way I can survive this mess is to change my address. The biggest lesson for me is to know when to throw my hands up, tap out, and get out of the ring.

Reflection

Do you know when to let go and walk away?

What activities or relationships do you continue to invest in that give you no return?

Do you know which battles are healthy and which are harmful?

Take Action

This month, evaluate what's working and what's not working in your life. Seek to understand why a decision or aspect in your life is or isn't working. For aspects in your life that aren't working, decide to either try something different or stop altogether. Some areas that you may want to evaluate include the following: relationships, career, finances, and health. For areas in your life that aren't working, create a plan to implement changes within the next three months.

36

BEST FRIENDS

....

If you have just one best friend in your lifetime, you
have been kissed by God and his infinite love.
—Shannon Jones

A BEST FRIEND LOVES YOU UNCONDITIONALLY.

They know your weaknesses and love you more.

They listen with opened ears, an opened heart, and a closed mouth.

They don't judge, only acknowledge. They also have the courage to tell you when you should have taken a different approach.

A best friend inspires you to be better, live wiser, and give more.

They see your faults and know that your faults only exist to keep you humble.

They see the best in you when you can only see the worst in you.

You can tell them your deepest secrets, and somehow, they try to melt the guilt away.

They understand your personality and fully accept you for who you are.

They know the language of your soul.

They pray and intercede on your behalf.

They are connected to you at a much deeper level.

If you are experiencing any of these qualities in a person, you are blessed beyond measure. Now that you know that you are blessed, it's your responsibility to appreciate the blessing.

Reflection

What would your life be like without this best friend?

Think of one experience that solidified your friendship with this best friend?

Take Action

Make a list of your friends and the qualities they possess.

Next, list actions you have taken to show your appreciation for their friendship.

This week, do something special for them to let them know that you value their friendship. You can send them a thank-you card, treat them to dinner, or give them a gift as a token of your appreciation.

37

BOOKS ARE MY FRIENDS

••••••••••••••••••••••••••••••

*A good book is like a best friend; the relationship
never gets old, no matter how many times you read it.*
—Shannon Jones

I AM MOST AT HOME AMONG BOOKS. YOU ARE MY FRIENDS. WE
have some of the best conversations. You listen to my heart and
my fears, and you feel my tears on your body. You never judge
me or shun me. You often stun me with their play on words.
(Oh, a pun.) I have experienced almost every emotion when
reading you—from joy, sorrow, and laughter to pain, sadness,
love, and madness. Once upon a time, this plethora of emotions
was reserved only for a man. I read your secrets and I tell you
mine. Sometimes we don't agree, but you remain kind. You never
get tired of me reading and needing you as you have the patience
of Job. Although I need you more, you need me too. You need
to be held, felt, heard, and preferred. I need to be understood,
reassured, cured, and matured. Thank you for indulging me in
this choreography of friendship.

'Til death do us part, we are joined at the hip. We get along so well after spending endless hours together. You have taken me to some of the world's most fascinating places. You've introduced me to both famous and unfamiliar faces. You've taught me so much With you, there's nothing I can't do. If I want to learn Mandarin, you are there to teach me that too. If I want to learn a new skill or just heal, you give me step-by-step instructions. I so value our time together, and I never want it to end. Dear librarian, I know you want me to go home, but I'm already there.

Reflection

When was the last time you read a good book?

What is your all-time favorite book?

What did you like most about this book?

Take Action

Set a goal to read more. If you don't read much currently, try reading a few minutes a day. You can even read short magazine articles. Eventually, try to work your way up to reading one book a month. Researchers at Yale University found that people who read live about two years longer than non-readers. According to the American Academy of Neurology, 32 percent of readers have a lower rate of mental decline compared to those who don't engage in reading. Researchers at Sussex University found that reading was more effective at fighting stress than listening to music, sipping a cup of tea, or even taking a walk. Reading can ease nerves by as much as 68 percent. It does not matter if the book is large or small; just read!

38

MISSION POSSIBLE

• •

Rest assured that the "mission" is on a mission to find
a missionary. Will you open the door when it knocks?
—Shannon Jones

THE MISSION FOUND YOU BECAUSE YOU HAVE THE TALENTS, COLLECTIVE
experiences, and relatability to carry out the mission. Your total
being makes the mission possible. Your mission is created from your
mess. Your mess serves as healing for others. The message may come
from unlikely places and unlikely experiences, but for likely reasons.
The reason is the 'why', and the 'why' creates the path for the mission
to find the missionary. A missionary goes beyond religion or religious
titles. It surpasses religious doctrine. A missionary is a person who
uses their life to support a mission or a cause.

The mission is more than possible. The question is, are you up
for the mission to be of service to others? We are the collective
consciousness and we each have a mission to complete. This
includes addressing racism, hunger, inequality, climate change,
feminism, human rights, poverty, health care, the penal system,
and every other -ism and system that is broken.

Reflection

What is your life's mission?

When you wake up every morning, what do you wish were different to benefit the human race, ecosystem, animal kingdom, etc.?

Take Action

Think of a time when you encountered a difficult experience, possibly an experience that created pain or embarrassment. Could that be your mission?

Think about a time when you saw an injustice being performed. How did that make you feel? Could that be your mission?

Think about where you can serve the greater good.

This week, look for organizations that you can get involved in to support your mission. Commit today to fulfilling a mission.

39

A BALANCED LIFE

• •

A tricycle has three wheels. A car has four
wheels. A balanced life has awareness.
—*Shannon Jones*

TO HAVE BALANCE, ONE MUST HAVE AWARENESS. BALANCE IS
critical for a harmonious life. Relationships are ripped apart
due to imbalances. Disease erodes the body due to imbalances.
Corporations go belly-up due to imbalances. An imbalance occurs
when there is an uneven distribution of something, creating a
disturbance. Test your balance:

Do you reprimand more than you praise?
Do you criticize more than you compliment?
Do you spend more than you make?
Do you talk more than you listen?
Do you depreciate more than you appreciate?
Do you give more than you take?

As a parent or supervisor, you can't reprimand more than you
praise, neither can you be afraid to reprimand. It's all a balancing

act. If a supervisor always gives praise to their employees and never provides constructive feedback, the employees will cease to grow and the supervisor would cease to perform.

We must be both.
Compassionate and stern.
A lion and a lamb.
A pillow and steel.

Reflection

Imagine your life as a seesaw. Is either side touching the ground? If so, you need to find balance.

What are two areas in your life that lack balance?

Take Action

This week, bring awareness to areas of your life that are out of balance.

On a sheet of paper, write down areas in your life that need balance. Some areas to consider are your work life, family life, and social life. For example, are you working twelve hours a day with little to no time to play, rest, and refuel?

Is your diet balanced to promote health and well-being? These are great areas to create balance.

40

THE SHUTDOWN

• •

> *If we listen, shutdowns teach us to sit down,*
> *slow down, and calm down so that we can*
> *shape up, show up, and turn up.*
> —*Shannon Jones*

FOR MOST, SHUTDOWNS ARE SEEN AS UNPLEASANT DISRUPTIONS. A shutdown can result from almost anything such as a loss of a job, a pandemic, or any other life event. A shutdown forces one to not be in control. It forces things to just be—to create space to do nothing; to ponder life; to sit and see; to watch and be; to observe what brings pain and pleasure; to measure daily treasures. Shutdowns stimulate creativity to brainstorm ways to utilize your gifts to earn a living. Shutdowns force us to sit down, slow down, and calm down so that we can shape up, show up, and turn up.

Reflection

Think about a time in your life when you faced uncertainty. You may have seen it as a problem or defeat, but when you shifted your mind, you realized that it offered the greatest life lesson.

Take Action

This week, examine a situation that you initially perceived as negative. After your examination, you may have realized that the situation wasn't as bad as you thought.

How did you shift your mind to find the silver lining? I'm not suggesting that you force the situation to be positive but consider the growth potential in the situation and how this situation has changed you for the better.

Don't miss life's greatest lessons by failing to find the silver lining. The silver lining offers a positive viewpoint in an otherwise negative situation.

41

HIDDEN

• •

No man is considered great until he is
willing to show the world his talent.
—Michelle A. Homme

YOU HAVE NOT MET ME, BUT YOU WILL. YOU SEE, I AM A BLESSING
in the making. I am hidden from the naked eye, but will one
day emerge from darkness into the light. I am nobody to you
now, but I will one day help you navigate your life. I can see
you, but you can't see me. I can see your confusion, conflict,
and capriciousness. I see your struggles with your life's purpose.
You are so focused on improving your weaknesses that you have
neglected your strengths. You are roaming in the wilderness
trying to find a place of belonging.

I am sent to help you find belonging within yourself. I am sent
to teach you how to invest in your strengths and monitor your
weaknesses. All the answers are within you—you just don't know
it yet. You have the strength to climb this mountain and the depth
to hit the ocean floor and float right back to the surface. You are
strong, resilient, and tenacious.

I am your life coach. You are my client. I will help you discover your true self as you help me fulfill my true purpose. Although I have no idea how we will meet or when we will meet, I am sure that my name has been spoken in the atmosphere and time will reveal my presence. I can't wait to meet you.

Reflection

You must believe that you have something to offer, even though your talents have not been revealed. What do you have to offer someone?

What do you have to offer a corporation?

What do you have to offer to a friendship?

Take Action

If you are searching to discover your strengths, talents, and gifts, take a personality assessment, such as *StrengthsFinder 2.0* or the Myers-Briggs Type Indicator. If you know what gifts and talents you possess, list how you will honor them daily.

42

DON'T BELIEVE EVERYTHING YOU SEE

. . . .

Never trust your beliefs any more than
you would an old eye prescription.
—Shannon Jones

ALTHOUGH MY EYEGLASS PRESCRIPTION IS TWO YEARS OLD, MY beliefs tell me that I can see just fine. I can see the trees, the birds, and the leaves—or so I think. Since I only see what I see, I don't know what I can't see.

I just got my new prescription, which has given me a fresh perspective, and I now see the shape of the leaves on the trees. I now see the majesty of the bird's crown which I couldn't see before. I now see the earth and all its splendor.

I feel silly that I had failed to consider that my vision was hindered. I thought I could see clearly when I could only see a silhouette. I have judged others by a silhouette. I have judged myself by a silhouette. I apologize for allowing my internal optics to distort my external world. Now I see. I am now open to listening. I am now open to learning. Due to my new perspective, I know that I am here to serve the trees, birds, and leaves and not judge what I can or cannot see.

Reflection

Our beliefs form our perceptions. Our perceptions form our perspectives, which is how we see the world; it is our outlook on life. Since our beliefs form what and how we think, we must ask ourselves whether our beliefs are limiting or empowering.

Do you need to change your beliefs? How will you change them? You change your beliefs by challenging them and then forming new beliefs.

Take Action

Have you ever formed a perception about a person or situation that was not true? This week, challenge limiting beliefs by asking yourself the following questions:

Why do I believe this?

Is this really true?

Is this a fair assessment of myself, the person, or the situation?

What are some new healthy beliefs I can form?

43

LIVE YOUR VALUES

....

I made an obligation to myself to live my life according
to my values and not by obligations imposed by society.
—Shannon Jones

WE EACH HAVE OBLIGATIONS. WE HAVE FAMILY OBLIGATIONS, parental obligations, career obligations, financial obligations, societal obligations, and so on. If we live our life by others' obligations, we spend our life living up to the expectations of others.

Obligations tell you that you can't live your dreams because you have children to raise. You can't indulge in experiences that make you happy because you have bills to pay. Obligations tell you that you can't pursue a second career because you waited too late. Obligations tell you that once you are hitched, your duty is to play the game of give and take. Until one day, you have nothing left to give and there's nothing left to take.

Your values are the true expression of yourself. They are the very things that get you excited about getting out of bed to start your day. Your values give your life meaning. They give you pleasure and eagerness. Values provide the framework for your purpose.

When you live life according to your values, your values start to showcase your value.

Honor your values today.

Reflection

What are your values?

Are you living your life by your values or by others' obligations?

Take Action

Take a moment to consider what you value. Write your values down and place them in a visible location where you can see them every day. Answer the following questions:

What gets me excited about life?

If I purchased three personalized T-shirts that are a true expression of me, what words and pictures would they express?

Your goal should be to honor at least one of your values each day. If you need additional assistance to identify your values, Dr. John DeMartini is a good resource. He authored the book *The Values Factor.*

44

LISTEN WITH THE HEART

. . . .

The heart listens to what the ears
hear but cannot comprehend.
—*Shannon Jones*

WE HEAR WITH OUR EARS, BUT WE LISTEN WITH OUR HEART. TRUE compassionate listening can only be heard through the heart. The heart knows what the ears can't hear. It listens to what is not being said. With this type of listening, the speaker is free to share childhood trauma and shameful drama and feel compassion as if he's talking to the Dalai Lama.

This type of listening is promiscuous, freely giving itself to anyone who wants it. It speaks to fear without ever saying a word. Because it knows that the outward expressions of anger, hatred, and bigotry are reflections of inward struggles of fear and trepidation.

This type of listening sees the pain and allows the speaker to pour out his soul to release the fountain of poison in his memory. As the speaker releases, he is cleansed a little bit more as he has come to know that he will not be judged. Instead, he will be loved, revered, and praised for his courage of vulnerability. As the speaker goes through the process of purging and detoxification, he gets better. He sees more clearly. The wounds are healing. He is now an earth angel. He is now the listener.

Reflection

Do you give your undivided attention to those who need it?

How do you feel when you share a painful story and the listener is fully present?

Take Action

This week, try to listen to someone's story actively and compassionately. Just listen. There is no need to try to fix the situation or problem; all they need is your heart. When you listen, be fully present and dismiss any judgment you have that may get in the way of the listening process.

45

CONTRADICTIONS

∙∙∙∙∙∙∙∙∙∙∙∙∙∙∙∙∙∙∙∙∙∙∙∙∙∙∙∙∙∙∙∙∙∙∙∙

Contradictions are meant to contradict themselves. When your thoughts are double-minded, you must remain single-minded.
—*Shannon Jones*

I AM WAITING, BUT NOT FORGOTTEN.
I am starving but not malnourished.
I am hidden, but transparent.
I am alone, but not lonely.
I am fragile but unbreakable.
I am in a dark place, but light is ever present.
I am confused, but I still know.
I am angry, but not bitter.
I feel guilt, but not shame.
I may not be right, but I'm also not wrong.
I have weaknesses, but my strengths overshadow them.

Reflection

Your thoughts are full of contradictions. One minute they tell you that you are worthy, then they change and tell you that you are not worth anything. One minute they call you a champion, then they call you a loser. You must know who you are and not let your thoughts define you.

Are you being controlled by your thoughts?

Take Action

The greatest way to control your thoughts is to exercise the following steps:

1. Become aware of your thoughts.
2. Once you are aware of them, observe what they are saying and what empowers them.
3. Challenge these thoughts.
4. Usher them out of your mind.

46

OPPORTUNITY

· ·

If opportunity knocks and you are scrambling
to put on your shoes, you don't deserve
the opportunity. Always be ready.
—Shannon Jones

OPPORTUNITY HAS ARRIVED AT MY DOORSTEP. WHERE ARE MY shoes? As I stroll to the door for Opportunity, Opportunity has left. It got tired of waiting.

Maybe it'll come back tomorrow. If it does, I'll surely be ready.

It comes the next day, but I am busy cleaning the dishes. After cleaning the dishes, I watch my favorite reality TV show. I need to walk the dog. I am so tired with all the running around that I don't want to do anything else. I don't even have the strength to open the door for Opportunity.

Maybe it'll come back tomorrow. If it does, I'll surely be ready.

I hear a knock at the door. It's only a person wanting directions. I have no time for her. I am waiting on Opportunity.

I'm waiting, but Opportunity doesn't knock on day three, four, or five. Weeks have turned into months and months into years since Opportunity had paid me a visit. Have I missed my opportunity?

I sit and wonder what my life would be like if I would have seized the opportunity. I now keep my shoes on. I outsource services that highjack my time.

I am now excited to give directions to a stranger because I know that Opportunity didn't come to receive directions but to give my life direction. Opportunity disguised itself to see if I would serve others so that it would serve me.

Reflection

Opportunities can be life-changing.

What was the last opportunity presented to you?

Did you take full advantage of the opportunity?

What will you do differently when Opportunity knocks again?

Take Action

We are presented with opportunities more often than we realize. It could be an opportunity for friendship, an opportunity to show kindness, or an opportunity to shift the trajectory of many generations to come. Throughout your day, look for these opportunities. When you look for opportunities, an awareness is created, which encourages them to show up.

47

BLUE JAY

• •

*Messages are given to us repeatedly. Each time they
call our name, the message is amplified. They come to
soothe us, warn us, and assist us. Are you listening?*
—*Shannon Jones*

BLUE JAY, WHAT DO YOU WANT? TWO OF YOU FLEW RIGHT IN
front of my car today. I saw two more just five days later. Why
do you travel in pairs? Your presence is majestic.

What do you represent? Your *color* represents creativity and
intelligence—strength and wisdom. Could you be telling me
that I have the wisdom and strength to get through this storm?
And that I have the intelligence and ingenuity to create a new life
for myself and my children?

The *crown* represents dignity and victory. Are you telling me that
although I don't feel victorious or dignified, I must hold my head
up high because victory is stalking my situation? Victory will
pursue my situation until it is victorious.

Your *wings* cover your body for protection and represent elevation. Could you be telling me that I am protected from danger and harm? And that I am in the valley now, but will be elevated in due season?

The number *two* represents strength in numbers and the importance of partnerships. Could it be that you travel in pairs to magnify this message times two to let me know that I am never alone?

You are so communicative, as you remind me that I am on the right path.

Reflection

Recall a time when you received the same message more than once. It could have been from a friend, an animal, a stranger, or a quiet voice. Did you realize that those words were not merely words but were messages to guide, encourage, and strengthen you?

Take Action

Get into a habit of communing with nature. Take a walk outdoors. Observe the birds, the trees, and the echoes of water. These activities will increase your awareness to help increase your ability to listen and receive messages.

48

ORDINARY PEOPLE
HAVE SUPERPOWERS

• •

Ordinary people possess superpowers. Ordinary people
are superheroes, and superheroes are ordinary people.
—*Shannon Jones*

SOME SUPERHEROES HAVE THE GIFT OF REGENERATION—HAVING
the ability to heal quickly.

Others have the gift of telekinesis—having the ability to move
things with one's mind.

Some exhibit clairvoyance—having the ability to see the unknown
as it is occurring.

Others have the ability of telepathy—having the power to read
people's minds.

Some superheroes have the gift of cognitive empathy—having the
ability to feel the emotions of another.

Others have the gift of precognition—having the ability to see the future.

The father who purchased the piece of land of little value thirty years ago had a gut feeling that one day that same piece of land would be worth millions. He had the gift of precognition.

The mother who felt that her son was in trouble, and soon after received a phone call from the hospital, had the gift of clairvoyance.

A stranger who displayed empathy as they could feel the pain of another, or the intercessor who interceded for the broken, wounded, and scorned, had the gift of cognitive empathy.

The friend who moved a mountain with their sincere prayers and faith exercised the gift of telekinesis.

The compassionate listener who allows those who are hurt to rid their hurts and burdens to heal has the gift of regeneration.

You see, ordinary people have superpowers. Ordinary people are superheroes.

Reflection

What are your superpowers?

Your superpowers are meant to be regifted. How are you regifting them?

Take Action

Your superpowers may not be as pronounced as the ones mentioned above but know that you have talents that are reserved for you and the people you are to assist.

This month, observe areas in your life that come easy. For example, are you great at organizing a party effortlessly? Or do you have amazing creative decorative strengths that make an economical room look like a million dollars?

Also, consider the over-the-top feedback you have received from others for doing what you deem as "ordinary" work.

49

DON'T TAKE IT TO
THE GRAVE

· ·

> *The graveyard is a storage unit for unused talents.*
> *Unlike most valuables, they can never be reclaimed.*
> —*Shannon Jones*

TALENTS SPEAK FROM THE GRAVE. YOU DID NOT FULFILL MY purpose. We had so much to offer to the world—from inventions, cures, fashions, and the arts. Together we could do anything. We could connect the dots to solve any problem. We had the skills and talents to dot every "I" and cross every "T" to find solutions.

Oh, how I wished we were self-starters, dream-seekers, and go-getters. We had the talent to be show-stoppers. Instead, we let fear stop our show. We were so occupied with reading other peoples' books that we failed to write our own. We were so busy admiring other peoples' works of art that we failed to recognize the artists in us.

We could have been so powerful together. Instead, we let fear come between our partnership. Now we are both stuck in this storage unit with nothing to do but sit and waste away.

Reflection

What are your talents?

Are you even using one-fourth of your talents?

What talents are you using?

Take Action

If you're unsure of the talents you possess, start looking today. Don't waste any more time. Don't take your talents to the grave. The grave can't use them.

If we look deep into past generations, we find that many of our ancestors failed to use their talents as well. Many of us may be dealing with ancestral karma. Ancestral karma is an ancestral blockage of physical and emotional energy patterns that has been passed down through generations. This karma may be creating blockages for you in discovering and living your highest potential. To address the ancestral karma, you must find the root cause of the karma and understand how this karma is preventing you from living up to your highest potential.

50

LOVE ME

•••••••••••••••••••••••••••••••••

Can you love me enough to judge your judgments
of me until your judgments turn into love?
—Shannon Jones

Judge me less. Love me more.
Judge me not. Love me unconditionally.
How can you not love me for whom you see?
And love thee who departed the Rea Sea.
I'm not perfect. Neither are you.
When I tell you my secrets, you judge those too.
Don't treat me like a reject. Nor dissect my faults.
Pray for my faults. Work on yours.
I have more to love. And less to judge.
Judge me not and love me more.

Reflection

Do you judge more than you love?

Who do you judge?

How would it feel to replace your judgment of them with love?

Take Action

Think of one person whom you judge often. Take a sheet of paper and fold it in half. On the top left side of the paper, write the word "Love." On the top right side of the paper, write the word "Judge." Write all the things that you love about that person on the left side of the paper. On the right side of the paper, write all the things that you judge and dislike about that person. Be intentional to be unbiased and fair in this activity. The goal is to come up with more things to love than judge.

51

LET IT GO
• •

Attachment Leads to Suffering.
—Buddha

ATTACH YOURSELF TO NOTHING AND NO ONE, NOT EVEN AN outcome. When you attach yourself to something or someone, you can't live life without it or them. And when it leaves you, you suffer. When you become attached to something or someone, you believe that it's yours. You feel that you own it. Ownership leads to greater responsibility of keeping it, which can lead to suffering.

Attachment to an outcome leads to disappointment. Instead, always give your best no matter the outcome. Attachment impairs your judgment as you cannot see things for what they are. It impairs your ability to see other opportunities as you see no greater opportunity than the one you have or want. Attachment limits your mobility to explore and be explored. It comes to exploit—exploit your life, your peace, your creativity. It robs you of your versatility. Attachment to a noun prohibits you from living in the now. Let go of what you feel you can't live without. This is the most freeing experience. Detach and choose to be free.

Reflection

What have you attached yourself to (e.g., material possessions, a relationship, an outcome, etc.)?

How can you enjoy or love something without attaching yourself to it?

Take Action

List three things that you cannot live without. Of course, these things should go beyond the essentials of water, food, and clothing. Some examples may include material possessions, certain friendships, or an outcome.

Now that you have your list of three things, create a goal that lessens your attachment to them. For example, if you are attached to an outcome of being on the *New York Times* best seller list as a book author, you have just created suffering from the stress of working to fulfill this expectation. If you don't fulfill this self-imposed expectation, disappointment will set in. Disappointment leads to suffering. The goal should be to write your book to help others, and not attach it to book sales or notoriety.

52

SHOW KINDNESS EVERY DAY

• •

> *Kindness is the language which the deaf*
> *can hear and the blind can see.*
> —*Mark Twain*

SHOWING KINDNESS IS A GREAT DAILY INTENTION. KINDNESS CAN BE expressed by performing the smallest acts, like giving a heartfelt compliment to a friend, family member, or stranger, or simply letting someone jump ahead of you in line to purchase goods. You can even show kindness by releasing a silent prayer to the person sitting next to you on an airplane. You can show kindness by sharing words of compassion. You can leave Post-it notes of inspiration or jump for joy to show appreciation. You can fix your kids a hearty breakfast before sending them off to school. You can tell a stranger that you hope they have a great day just before the elevator doors close. You can surprise a friend with concert tickets. You can show kindness by buying the local firefighters' icy slushies on a hot summer day.

Start today to show kindness every day. You can show kindness in a big or small way. It doesn't matter, as long as you give it away, every single day.

Reflection

When was the last time you showed kindness to someone?
How did you show kindness?

When was the last time someone showed kindness to you?

Take Action

Today, show kindness to someone. The following are just a few ideas to show kindness:

Surprise a family member with dinner.
Tell a friend that you appreciate them for being a good listener.
Thank your kids for allowing you to have a moment of quiet time.
Buy groceries for a stranger while in line at the grocery store.
Send a card to a friend for no special occasion.

Try to set an intention every day to show kindness in some way.

53

THE CLAY TALKS TO
THE POTTER

• •

Trust the potter. He's made a name for himself.
—*Shannon Jones*

DEAR POTTER, I AM TIRED, WORRIED, AND WEAK. THE STRETCHING is causing me pain in my muscle, joints, and feet. I'm dizzy from all this spinning. On this wheel, I'm losing my mind and my hair is thinning. I want off this wheel. This is my last and final plea. Please listen to me and just let me be.

Dear clay, you may be spinning out of control, but don't fold. I'm making you into an original, not a mold. Toughen up and enjoy the ride; soon you will thrive.

Just the right amount of pressure is applied so that you are not set aside but are qualified and not denied. You see, this is the application process of life. Can you trust your intuition, the wheel's mission? Most of all, can you trust my vision?

I envision a beautiful masterpiece—fit for a king.

I'm stretching and pulling you in all the right places, from all corners and all angles so that you endure life's tangles and snares, with minor cuts, scrapes, and tears.

I'm pulling out strife, pride, and envy—and replacing it with lucidity, empathy, and tenacity.

Don't resist. Flexibility is necessary for your upward mobility. If you resist, you will break, causing future hostility.

Dear clay, I know you're spinning out of control, but little do you know it's making you whole.

Reflection

In what areas are you being challenged in your life?

Take Action

Try imagining how your current situation is creating growth. You may be experiencing pain and fear, but you are also learning and getting stronger. It's in life's challenges that we are strengthened.

This month, plan to take a pottery class so that you can see firsthand how the process of challenge and discomfort creates beauty.

54

STOP, REST, AND BREATHE

• •

Life is full of upward and downward hills. Climbing
steep hills requires you to stop, rest, and breathe. If
you can make it up, going down requires little effort.
—*Shannon Jones*

YOU CAN DO IT. THE CLIMB MAY BE HARD, BUT YOU CAN DO IT.
The hills may be steep, but you can do it. You will slip and lose
your grip. But don't give up. You may even fall two feet down
but get back up. Settle down, rest, and take a deep breath. Don't
panic. If you can make the climb up, going down will be a breeze.
Remember, it's always harder going up. If your head stays in the
game, the body will follow. If the mind can do it, the body won't
quit. You will strengthen your mental stamina if you don't look
back but look up. You've got this. You can make it if you don't
give up as you go up.

Reflection

What has been your hardest climb (physically or emotionally)? What tools did you use to get to the top or complete the task?

Take Action

In life's toughest times, practice stopping, resting, and breathing. For example, if you're having a disagreement with someone, stop and pause before you respond. If you're experiencing anxiety about a situation, stop, rest, and breathe. These tools will help you catch your breath, and they will create self-awareness so that you will not react to life but instead respond to it. A reaction is emotionally charged and thoughtless, whereas a response is intentional and mindful.

55

THREE-LEGGED DOG

• •

Let your differences chase opportunities
and tackle limitations.
—Shannon Jones

THERE ARE TWO WHITE DOGS. THEY LOOK THE SAME. THEY BOTH run through the jungle and leap through rice fields. They swim like sea turtles embracing the current. They're happy and carefree. They're curious and exploratory. They love people. They horseplay and downward dog. They climb uphill at sundown.

Wait, they are not the same. One has a scar on its right ear. The biggest difference is that one dog only has three legs. How is it that the three-legged dog can do everything that the four-legged dog can do? Maybe it doesn't see its differences. Maybe it only sees its similarities. Maybe it sees that it has three legs versus one missing—it has more legs than fewer. It doesn't see its difference as a limitation but rather as inspiration.

Reflection

What is one thing that you wish you could change about yourself?

Why would you change it?

Take Action

On a sheet of paper, write three things that capture the beauty in what you would change about yourself. The purpose of this exercise is to help you embrace what you perceive as a shortcoming. Once you identify the beauty, your perception of this shortcoming will hopefully shift so that you will see it as a superpower. This is the epitome of self-acceptance, and ultimately, self-love.

56

DOG STUCK IN MUD

• •

We will each get stuck during this lifetime. Be sure to
surround yourself with people who can pull you out.
—*Shannon Jones*

If you were religion, you would tell the dog to pray for help.

If you were optimism, you would tell the dog to hang in there.

If you were pessimism, you would tell the dog to start digging its own grave.

If you were judgment, you would ask the dog what it did to get there.

If you were hatred, you would ask the dog what you need to do to keep it there.

If you were spirituality, you would tell the dog to meditate.

If you were chauvinism, you would ask the dog its gender.

If you were a business owner, you would ask the dog how much it's willing to pay to get out.

If you were rain, you would clean it up.

If you were *kind*, you would reach down and pull it out.

Reflection

What do you do when you are stuck?

Do you have a few people in your life who care about you to help you up?

What do you do when a friend is stuck?

Are you a go-to resource to give someone a hand up?

Take Action

This week, send a thank-you text to a person who pulled you up. Thank them for being a great and trusted friend. If you have pulled someone up, text them to see how they are doing. Many times, just letting a person know that you are thinking of them helps them get or stay unstuck.

57

I JUST DON'T KNOW
• •

When you don't know, trust that life does.
—Shannon Jones

I DON'T KNOW WHERE I'M GOING. I'VE NEVER BEEN ON THIS ROAD before. Nothing looks familiar. It seems that I'm on this road all alone. I've passed only a few cars, all going in the opposite direction. There is nothing but trees, grass, and leaves. The towns are getting smaller while people's biases are growing larger. Fear grips me as I realize I am not safe. I pass through enough towns, then I finally reach a city.

Things are finally starting to look familiar. I see familiar landmarks and street signs. I see other cars that are going in my direction. This is my community, until I realize that I still don't know where I'm going. Is this where I'm supposed to be? How is it that I'm not lost anymore, but I still don't know where I'm going? I am not full of fear, but I still don't feel safe. I am grateful, but I don't feel so great.

At this age and stage, I should know exactly where I'm going. But instead, I feel lost and confused. I feel trapped and can't find any clues to this mundane life of mine. It's Monday morning again and I am still uninspired. I wish I could retire and hire myself to work for my own destiny. I believe that one day I will know my path and work for my destiny—maybe not today, but eventually.

Reflection

Have you ever been certain that you knew where you were going, but when you arrived it was not what you thought it would be?

Do you feel accomplished at times and like a failure at other times?

Take Action

This week, create strategies to release fear by embracing the uncertainty, with the hope that things will get better.

Think of one area in your life that creates a feeling of confusion and uncertainty. On a sheet of paper, answer the following questions:

What areas in my life do I feel the most lost?
What emotions resonate with me when I am confused and living in uncertainty?
How do I embrace the unknown?

58

MARINARA SAUCE

•••••••••••••••••••••••••••••••

Life is like a basic sauce. You can keep it simple or
make it as elaborate as you wish. Chef your life.
—*Shannon Jones*

MARINARA SAUCE IS ONE OF THE SIMPLEST SAUCES TO MAKE. ALL
you need are tomatoes, olive oil, and fresh garlic flakes. With
a basic marinara sauce, you can make a meaty Bolognese sauce
served to-go or create a tasty sloppy joe. Add a cup of liquor to
create a vodka sauce. To turn your vodka sauce into a fra diavolo
sauce, add a tablespoon of red pepper flakes.

To sum it up, a lot can be made from three basic ingredients.
Don't just look at the three. Instead, see how you can multiply
the three to create what you want your life to be. But you must
first appreciate the three to create your life of jubilee.

Reflection

A chef is the king of their kitchen. A great chef masters spices and ingredients. They know what pairs well with certain foods. They create new concoctions because they take risks. How can you "chef" your life?

Take Action

What does "chef-ing" your life mean to you? It may mean that you must first identify your raw talents, then identify your dreams. On a sheet of paper, write your talents on the left side of the paper and your dreams on the right side of the paper. When you see your talents and goals side by side, how do your talents support your goals, and vice versa?

Do you need to strengthen your talents?

Do you need to take a few classes or improve on a few soft skills?

Do you need to expand your friend group?

59

THE FIXER-UPPER

•••••••••••••••••••••••••••••••••

*If every problem has a solution, what
problem were you born to fix?*
—Shannon Jones

WHAT WERE YOU BORN TO FIX? COULD IT BE THAT YOU WERE BORN
to promote racial equality by changing policies and police brutality?
Were you born to love apples, thus creating the technological
castle just thirteen hours from Seattle? Were you born to be a $50
million comedic prodigy and walk away from it all because staying
in the business no longer created laughter or the happily-ever-
after? Were you born to give people hope through *O* magazine
and showcase your acting diversity in *The Color Purple* scenes? Like
Nelson Mandela, were you born to dismantle the apartheid and
shed light on the great divide and political genocide?

What if we were more interested in how we could fix a broken
world more than succeeding in the world? We would have
reversed climate change. We would have ended hunger. Poverty
would not be the majority and being white would not be the
supreme authority.

We were all born to fix a broken world and heal a broken heart. We must each do our part.

Reflection

Ponder things that you care about and take action to lessen inequities and disparities. For example, are you passionate about educational equality, food security, or equality of opportunity?

Take Action

Find a cause to stand for today. Find a cause that gives you passion. Martin Luther King Jr. once said, "A man who does not have something for which he is willing to die is not fit to live."

Your job this week is to discover what you were born to fix. Do it with passion, as if your life depends on it.

60

SURVIVING THE IN-BETWEEN

· ·

The beginning is exciting, the end is
carefree, the in-between is a raging fire.
—*Shannon Jones*

I CAN GET MARRIED, BUT DO I HAVE WHAT IT TAKES TO BE A GOOD partner? I can have children, but can I be a great parent? I can enroll in college, but do I have the stamina to graduate? I can get a job, but can I thrive in my job until it becomes a career? I can start writing a book, but can I complete it?

Can the marriage last through the fights and snares until our hearts reunite? Can I raise the children to be self-sufficient and kind so that they raise me when I am old? Can I earn the degree, and do I have what it takes to make it through the in-between? Can I enjoy my career? Do I have what it takes to finish, publish, and sell books with no platform?

In the in-between, there is total exhaustion as it is the longest journey. It is the journey of a million miles and counting. It's full of uncertainty and pain. Dysfunction thrives in the in-between.

The in-between is full of questions with few answers. You're in the thick of life—so thick that it feels like you're swimming in milk.

In the in-between, there is pressure from all sides. You feel like you're in a pressure cooker. The cooker is whistling as the steam needs to escape. With time, the steam will escape, and before long you'll be helping someone else through their in-between.

Reflection

What stage are you experiencing in your life?

What life lessons have you learned?

Take Action

Part of surviving the in-between is to know that you are in it. It is also important to understand that this may be the toughest season of life, but like all seasons, it will pass. The in-between may not create laughter now, but hopefully parts of it will later.

Journaling is a great way to capture and remember the in-between moments.

What aspects of this season are you enjoying?

This week, incorporate more of these enjoyable aspects. Incorporating more enjoyable aspects of this season helps mitigate the pressure.

61

PEOPLE CAN'T GIVE YOU WHAT THEY DON'T HAVE

· ·

> *People can't give you what they don't have. If they*
> *had it, they'd give it. It has nothing to do with you,*
> *but everything to do with what they don't have.*
> —*Shannon Jones*

WHEN I ASK YOU TO GIVE ME $100, YOU ONLY GIVE ME $10.
When I ask you to give me attention, you only ignore.
When I ask you to give me a meal, you give me nothing.
When I ask you for hope, you give me despair.
When I ask you for a hug, you suffocate.

You gave me $10 'cause that's all you have.
You ignored me 'cause you are emotionally deaf.
You gave me nothing to eat 'cause you are malnourished.
You gave me despair 'cause you feel hopeless.
You suffocate 'cause you are gasping for acceptance.

Now I know that you can't give me what you don't have. I believe
if you could, you would. I realize that you need to heal. Because

of this insight, I am no longer angry with you. I forgive you. Now go heal so that you can give a little more to yourself than you gave me.

Reflection

Are you angry with someone who you feel didn't give you what you needed or deserved?

Do you know what you need and want?

Are you giving yourself what you need, want, and deserve?

Take Action

If you are angry because you are not getting what you need from others, identify how you can supply this need for yourself. For example, if you love to travel and your partner doesn't, figure out how you can travel without your partner and release anger before it turns to resentment. This is your life. Take personal responsibility for your life and create your own happiness.

62

MEDITATION IS MY
BEST FRIEND

• •

> *When I meditate, I breathe in all of your goodness,*
> *peace, and love. I breathe out all the toxins and*
> *stress. Sometimes a feeling of euphoria comes over me.*
> *It's indescribable. No other friend or lover has ever*
> *given me this satisfaction. You are my best friend.*
> —*Shannon Jones*

EVERYONE AND EVERYTHING WANTS SOMETHING FROM ME.

The car runs well but it still requires quarterly oil changes.

My job requires me to grow the business and provide exceptional customer support.

My team requires me to hold them accountable.

My children require me to provide food, shelter, and everything else in between.

My book club buddies require me to read and discuss books.

My body requires food and water.

My friends require me to provide emotional support.

My dog requires care and daily walks.

My house requires routine maintenance and repairs.

Meditation is the only thing that requires nothing of me. It doesn't require me to utter a word. It doesn't even require me to think. It is my refuge from the storm. It relieves me from stress, anxieties, and all sorts of calamities. I can totally be myself. It requires the least of me, yet it gives me the most. The only thing it wants from me is to be still. As I breathe, it breathes life into me. It gives me peace. It heals my body. It supports my well-being. It truly knows what's best for me. Meditation is my best friend.

Reflection

Have you ever meditated?

Do you know the benefits of meditation?

Take Action

Research has confirmed a plethora of scientific benefits of meditation. A study conducted by UCLA found that long-term meditators had better-preserved brains than non-meditators as they age. A review study conducted by Johns Hopkins found that mindfulness meditation has the ability to reduce symptoms of depression, anxiety, and pain. A Harvard study founded that mindfulness mediation can actually change the structure of the brain by increasing the cortical thickness in the hippocampus, which governs learning and memory.

For the next five days, incorporate fifteen minutes of meditation into your day. It is best to meditate first thing in the morning to create mindfulness as you start your day. If it's difficult to incorporate in the morning, try to incorporate some time throughout the day. There are several free apps to help you create a structure for meditation. In the beginning, it may be difficult for you to focus, but stick to a routine.

63

SERVE OTHERS

• •

If you serve God with all your heart and do not
serve your fellow neighbor, you are not upright. As
a matter of fact, you are a downright hypocrite.
—*Shannon Jones*

THE TRUE MEASURE OF SERVICE IS NOT OUR SERVICE TO GOD BUT
our service to others. When you serve others, you serve God.

Likewise, we love God by loving others. In turn, God shows us
love by others loving us.

It is impossible to serve God without serving others. It is impossible
to love God without loving others.

Even our gifts and talents are for the service of others. God blesses
us through people. He restores us through people and guides us
through people. People are the link to experiencing God. To
experience the fullness of God, you must have an appetite for
people.

If you want to serve God, serve people. If you love God, show love to others. If you want to show God respect, take care of the earth and the environment.

The human experience is about being humane. It's about ushering the continuous flow of compassion for all beings. Serving God is about serving others. Loving God is about loving people.

Reflection

Who did—or who will—you serve today?

Take Action

Today, create an intention of who you will serve. Try to serve someone you wouldn't normally serve. These actions can be small acts of service such as opening a door or helping a coworker with a project. Try to serve someone daily until you establish a new normal of serving others.

64

"YET" IS A CHAMELEON

....

> *"Yet" creeps up on you without any announcement.*
> *It doesn't look anything like you expected,*
> *but "yet" the manifestation appears.*
> —*Shannon Jones*

"YET" IS AN ASSURANCE THAT YOU WILL OBTAIN YOUR DESIRES sooner or later, if you haven't already. The hope that things will get better, even if it gets worse. The assurance that whatever is broken will be fixed, even if it is cracked. The assurance that whatever is injured will be healed, even if it is bruised or scarred. Be cognizant that the outcome may not look as you had expected. Situations and circumstances come to strengthen our character and make us better which may not resemble growth or recovery. When a lamp is cracked or damaged, it can still provide light. When someone is injured, they can still perform a duty.

"Yet" gives hope that even though it hasn't happened yet, it will occur. Time has to be created for what has been spoken into the universe. What has been spoken has already manifested in the universe. It's now waiting to appear on earth. Never underestimate the power of "yet" and its many faces, shapes, colors, and appearances.

Reflection

Could it be possible that you've already received what you've been awaiting?

The manifestation and path may look different from what you had expected. Be open to the unfamiliar and unexpected.

Take Action

Take inventory of your dreams and desires. Some of your dreams and desires may have already manifested. The manifestation may not look as you had expected. For example, if you desire to be a mentor, guru, and advisor, it's likely that you already serve in these roles. Think about people whom you advise. More likely than not, this desire of mentorship has been manifested in your life. You may not recognize it as you may have expected a leadership title or position to accompany this role of mentorship.

65

CARDINALS DELIVER LOVE LETTERS

••••••••••••••••••••••••••••••••••

When you see a cardinal, know that someone is
blowing kisses to you. It visits you to tell you that
you are loved by someone or something somewhere.
—*Shannon Jones*

OH, YOU SING SO LOVELY. YOU HAVE SUCH A BEAUTIFUL VOICE. Your pitch is perfect. The melody is so harmonious. You can sing! You are a songwriter and songster. Your performance is a masterpiece.

If only I knew what you were saying. Given your red color, your presence is the epitome of love. You exude creativity and fascination. Your presence is so warming and reassuring. You are so graceful and unassuming. You are so peaceful and tranquil.

As you sing, I imagine you wrote this song especially for me. I am convinced that you are telling me just how much I am loved. You are telling me that I am much more creative than I think—that my creativity can help me create the life I want. Your lyrics inform me that I can captivate many with my warm smile and heart. You are assuring me that I have swag and elegance to move any room. And that although my performance doesn't look anything like yours, it can deliver love better than any postmaster delivering mail. You remind me that the peace I feel in your presence is the same peace others feel in mine. Although my voice will never be as lovely as yours, the love that I give to myself helps me find my voice.

Reflection

When was the last time you saw a cardinal?

Do you create daily intentions to show love?

Take Action

This week, try to walk in nature at least two times. While you are walking, listen and look. Observe all the animals that you see. These observations will increase your awareness of nature, which will also increase your awareness in other areas of your life. Birds and animals have a way of serving as messengers to help us connect pieces to life's puzzles. When we bask in nature, they show us the nature of love so that we can give and receive love. As you commune with nature, you just might see a cardinal.

66

WE LEARN WHAT WE LOVE, AND WE LOVE WHAT WE LEARN
••••••••••••••••••••••••••••••••••

Show me what you've learned, and
I will tell you what you love.
—*Shannon Jones*

WHAT YOU SPEND YOUR TIME LEARNING IS WHAT YOU WILL perfect. If you say you love your job, what new information have you acquired to improve your performance? If you say you love your talent, what have you done to strengthen it? If you say you love your partner, they shouldn't be a stranger. If you say you love yourself, who are you? If you say you love reading, what book are you currently reading? If you say you love giving, when was the last time you gave of yourself and your time? If you say you want to be the best athlete, how often do you practice? If you say you want to be a great student, how much time do you spend studying and learning? If you say you love peace, when was the last time you pursued peace in an argument? If you say you love people, when was the last time you showed kindness?

When you love something, you are curious to learn more about it—you ask great questions. We learn what we love, and we love what we learn.

Reflection

What do you love? What have you learned? Are your responses to these two questions congruent in your life? Be honest with yourself.

Take Action

This week, examine what you've learned and are learning. Ponder if you are enjoying learning about it. What questions have you asked to facilitate the learning process? This activity should help you eliminate areas in your life in which you lack passion to identify areas that give you excitement.

67

GROUND YOURSELF

••••••••••••••••••••••••••••••••

The ground grounds your body in a way that gets
you dirty so that your mind becomes clean.
—*Shannon Jones*

WHEN YOU ARE GROUNDED, YOU ARE ROOTED IN SOMETHING larger than yourself. Your roots attach to the earth with such a force that you become the earth and the earth becomes you. Similar to how a palm tree is grounded by the riverbank which sways and bends with strong winds, but it will not break because it's rooted in the earth.

Ground yourself in the earth. Ground yourself in dirt. There is something about dirt that cleanses. It cleanses the body and mind better than any soap, detergent, or dishwashing liquid. Dirt is cooling and captivating. When your feet encounter dirt, grass, water, soil, sand, and land, you gain a sense of jubilation just from the sensation. Earthing is said to heal the body of ailments. It's been proven to remove pressure, inflammation, and aggravation. It also removes stress and tightness in your chest.

To enjoy the benefits, all you need to do is walk barefoot on earth. Leave your shoes behind and place your feet in the dirt. It won't cost you anything because the ground is free. Give it a try. Earth until you and earth unify.

Reflection

Do you resemble the palm tree where your feet are set and fixed in the ground, both physically and mentally?

Do you know the benefits of grounding or earthing?

Take Action

A study in the Journal of Alternative and Complementary Medicine reported that participants slept better when they were grounded and also reported a reduction in pain and stress. Another study in the Journal of Alternative and Complementary Medicine reported that earthing or grounding reduced cardiovascular risk in participants. According to a study published in the Journal of Inflammation Research, when you ground, mobile electrons from the Earth make contact with your skin and enter your body, acting as natural antioxidants, protecting cells, tissue, and organs from oxidative stress.

Today, plan to walk around barefooted in the dirt, grass, soil, or sand. You can also walk alongside the beach, lake, or river, and let the water and sand glide through your toes. Try to practice grounding regularly.

68

ABOUNDING IN ABUNDANCE

• •

*Abundance is like swimming in a body of water
that has no dead ends, only unlimited possibilities.*
—*Shannon Jones*

PICTURE YOURSELF EATING AT AN ALL-YOU-CAN-EAT BUFFET Restaurant—not just any all-you-can-eat buffet restaurant, but one that serves food from every culture. One that whets the appetite for both carnivores and omnivores. A restaurant that satisfies the palates of meat-lovers, vegetarians, and vegans. This restaurant serves all your childhood favorites. It serves your favorite holiday meals. The buffet table is endless.

Imagine that life is an endless buffet where you're satisfied with the offerings. You are satisfied with the service and with the variety. You can feast on these delectable offerings in good company—in the company of friends and loved ones. You love what you do. You are living your life to the fullest with passion and excitement. You are assisting and serving others. Picture yourself eating at an all-you-can-eat buffet called life. Picture yourself living in a state of abundance as abundance is a state of mind.

Reflection

In what areas of your life are you experiencing abundance? For example, are you experiencing abundance in your relationships, career, business, finances, etc.? If you're experiencing abundance in these areas, your mind experienced it first.

Take Action

This month, visit an all-you-can-eat buffet. When you walk into the restaurant, envision your life resembling the buffet. Observe what feelings resonate within you when you see this outward image of abundance. Once you shift your mind from a state of lack to a state of abundance, you will start to feast on the unlimited offerings of life.

69

VISIONING EXERCISE

••••••••••••••••••••••••••••••••••••••

> *See yourself immersed in the life you want, and*
> *the life you want will emerge into your reality.*
> —*Shannon Jones*

CLOSE YOUR EYES AND IMAGINE THAT YOU ARE ATTENDING YOUR twenty-year high school reunion. You look and feel fabulous! Envision the outfit you are wearing. How does it look on you? How was your hair styled? Is it short, long, or bobbed? You have entered the ballroom. Who are you talking to? They comment on how great you look. They ask you, "What have you been doing for the past twenty years?" They ask if you are happy. How will you answer these questions? What passions will you share? Share the wonderful person you have become. Speak about your dreams that came true and the great life you have built that supports your well-being. Again, envision that you are currently living the life of your dreams. Make this exercise as real as possible, as if it already happened, until you become overwhelmed with joy.

Now open your eyes.

Reflection

During this exercise, what emotions did you experience?
What gave you great joy?
Did this experience feel real to you?
What made it feel real?

Take Action

On a sheet of paper, write down this visioning exercise. For example, write how you looked, what you were wearing, and how you felt. Write down this life as if you are living it today. Read aloud this visioning exercise daily until this exercise is recognized as your life.

70

DOGS "TAIL" THE TRUTH
•••••••••••••••••••••••••••••••••

The truth is present when you live in the present.
—Shannon Jones

DOGS LIVE IN THE PRESENT. THEIR PRESENCE IS PLAYED OUT IN their tail. Dogs don't lie because their tail keeps them honest. It's like a built-in accountability partner. It can only speak truth. It is so real and authentic; it can't pretend. Talk about wearing your feelings on your sleeve; they wear theirs on their tail.

They show you when they are excited and alert. Their tail exhibits broad strokes when they are happy and short strokes when they are nervous. You know when they submit versus resist. If you want to know their mood, look at their tail. A dog's tail always tells the truth.

Because dogs live in the present, their emotions are consistent and reliable. Their expressions and emotions are experienced in the present. They don't live in the past or exhibit past expressions. They don't express excitement from yesterday's thrills; it's the past. Their expressions are real and are in real-time.

Dogs always "tail" the truth.

Reflection

Have you ever observed a dog's behavior? The wag of its tail is insightful.

Think about your varied emotions. Are your emotions based on past experiences or concern for the future?

Take Action

Starting today, create an awareness of your thoughts. Most thoughts are generated from the past and future. Therefore, our thoughts do not reflect the present moment. Many times, thoughts of the past create regret and bitterness, and thoughts of the future create anxiety of what might happen. Therefore, many past and future thoughts create negative emotions.

Fill your left arm with loose rubber bands, about ten of them. Every time you catch yourself thinking about the past or future, transfer a rubber band from your left arm to your right arm. The purpose of this exercise is to create awareness of your thoughts. The goal is to reduce negative thoughts by creating awareness of your thoughts and training the brain to live in the present. At the end of this exercise, the goal is to have more rubber bands on your left arm, which reflects living in the present. Repeat this exercise several times a day until living in the present becomes second nature.

71

THE RHYTHM OF LIFE
••••••••••••••••••••••••••••••••••

Watching a person dance offbeat is painful to
witness. It's like watching a person live their life
uncontrollably and disorderly. There is an effortless
groove to life when you catch the rhythm.
—*Shannon Jones*

WAVES IN AN OCEAN FLOW WITH EASE. THEY FULFILL THEIR
purpose as they create ripple effects for all to see. They don't try
to be anything else but that which they were created to be. There's
a rhythm to their flow. There's a rhythm to life. They seem to
know when to thrive and when to stay calm. They often flow in
unison because they are one. Even when they crash, they're still
on one accord, as cymbals create a crashing sound that embodies
harmony.

How can my life be a wave? A wave where I see my beauty and
execute my purpose. Where I catch the rhythm of my life and
flow with the current rather than against it. I want my life to flow
with ease on the path of least resistance.

How can my life be a wave? Where I know that I am exactly where I'm supposed to be at this present moment and dismiss thoughts that I'm frozen in time. How can I be a wave, where I let it happen instead of making it happen? How, like the wave, do I let go, and go with the flow?

I now know who I am. I am the wave. I am now comfortable in my own skin as the waves are comfortable in their oceanic vessel. I now ride the waves of life. Wherever it takes me, I will go. I now go where it takes me, knowing that the wave has a sense of direction and cosmic intelligence.

Reflection

Are you grooving to life or are you dancing offbeat? Grooving to the beat of life may involve having supportive relationships that challenge your growth and development.

Are there any areas of your life that you are resisting? If so, why are you resisting this part of your life?

Take Action

What action steps do you need to take to get into the rhythm of your life?

What does "getting" into the rhythm and flow look like for you? For example, does it look like getting rid of what no longer serves you, such as a relationship, a job, harmful activities, etc.?

72

COUNT YOUR BLESSINGS
••••••••••••••••••••••••••••••••••

When we add up the days, our blessings
outnumber our misfortunes. If it weren't true,
we wouldn't be alive to even count them.
—Shannon Jones

BLESSINGS VISIT ME EVERY MORNING. THE SUN SHINES BRIGHT IN my window. It gives me a morning kiss bigger than any partner could give.

Blessings visit me every morning. My legs perform for morning walks.

Blessings visit me every morning. The gentle breeze of whispers from the wind meets me as I venture into nature.

Blessings visit me every morning. I have healthy food to nourish my body.

Blessings visit me every morning. The food I have may not be the healthiest, but it still gives me life.

Blessings visit me every morning. My children knock on my door and grace me with gigantic hugs and kisses.

Blessings visit me every morning. I am in my own bed and not on the street or in a hospital.

Blessings visit me every morning. I may be on the street or in a hospital, but I am alive.

Blessings visit me every morning. I have my own hair to comb and do not have to be reminded of the devastating effects of chemotherapy.

Blessings visit me every morning. Although I have no hair to comb today, my hair follicles hold the power of regeneration. My hair will grow back.

Blessings visit me every morning. I have a family. Some people have no one.

Blessings visit me every morning, although I have no one, I am someone special.

I could go on and on and on. There is no number that can capture your blessings because they are infinite. Whenever you can't think of a blessing, accept a kiss from the sun. Accept a whisper in your ear from the wind. When you want to be reminded of your many blessings, grab your head and be thankful for a sober mind, even if it's only as you read this book.

Reflection

What blessings are you grateful for?

Why are you grateful for these blessings?

Take Action

Tomorrow morning, start counting your blessings and record them in a gratitude journal. Start counting them from the time you wake up until the time you go to bed, for just one day. Don't forget to count waking up as your first blessing.

73

NEVER MIND THE PLACE; JUST MEDITATE

. . . .

Meditation is transportable. No need for a
suitcase because all you need is you.
—Shannon Jones

MEDITATION IS A STATE OF MIND AND A STATE OF BEING. IT'S A state of inner silence when there is external chaos. It travels through the mind similar to how my body travels by air, train and car. It is a place of peace when your life is filled with war, bickering, and arguments. It's solitude when people fill your space every hour of the day. At the same time, it is a place of companionship when you are lonely.

When I am too busy to think straight, meditation removes all thought. When my brain is drained, it fills me with nothing. When my mind is in a constant state of chitchat, it nurtures me with silence.

Meditation is a state of mind and a state of being. No matter where I am or what I'm doing, I take it with me wherever I go.

Reflection

You can meditate anywhere. Meditation is the presence of mindfulness. Meditation is thoughtless awareness.

What are some daily activities where you can create mindfulness without thought? For example, when you are performing chores, focus on performing that chore in the present moment. Try not to think about anything.

Take Action

Sit in a comfortable position. Now plant the seed of intention that your mind and body are open to the experience of meditation wherever it takes you.

Place your hands on your lap. Start to follow your breath. Don't think about anything, just follow your breath. Guess what? You are meditating. Continue to keep your awareness on your breath. Breathe in slowly, then out slowly. If your mind starts to wander, center yourself by following your breath. Do this for fifteen minutes.

74

ALL IS "WELL"

• •

I am well enough to know that living a life
of well-being makes all things well.
—*Shannon Jones*

MY GOAL IN THIS LIFETIME IS TO BE WELL.

I want to be well-informed. Informed enough to know who I am and that who I am is enough.

I want to have well intentions. I want to know I can have my heart's desires, if my desires are well-hearted.

I want to be well-off. I want to have enough affluence to influence the weak and needy.

I want to hear the words "well done," to know that I did my part in the global community.

I want to live a life of well-being because it's in the *being* that makes all things well.

I want to be well-traveled. Well-traveled to connect with people from different backgrounds and cultures, knowing that our similarities connect us.

I want to be well-connected. Well-connected to know that there is a global disconnect within the human species that requires immediate attention.

I want to be well-received. Well-received to be fully supported and accepted when I accept and fully support others.

I want to be well-rounded. Well-rounded enough to make necessary self-adjustments to soften the rough edges.

I want to be well-equipped. Well-equipped to know that I will have the necessary resources if I serve as a resource.

I want to be well-built. Well-built to know that I am made with high quality, but humble enough to know that I am no better than anyone else.

All is well, and well is all.

Reflection

We should all strive to live a life of well-being. We should each strive for wellness to saturate every part of our life.

Is your mind and body full of wellness?

Do you strive to ensure that your thoughts are well and positive?

Take Action

From the collection above, circle three "well" words that you would like to focus your attention on this week. For example, if you circled the word "well-being," what steps are you going to take to strengthen well-being in your life?

75

ASK FOR WHAT YOU WANT

••••••••••••••••••••••••••••••••••••

I am worthy and deserving enough to receive exactly
what I ask for. If not, I have the right to walk away.
—Shannon Jones

IF YOU WANT SOMETHING, ASK FOR IT. YOU ARE WORTHY OF
receiving exactly what you ask for. If your desires support you
and serve others, you have every right to expect to receive what
you've asked for. Give yourself permission to receive. When you
make a formal request of your wants and desires, you are notifying
the giver to release the gift.

A formal request activates the transaction. When you fail to ask
for what you want, you are living in a state of limitations. You fail
to ask because you don't believe that you are worthy enough to
receive your desires or feel that someone else is more deserving.
In the state of abundance, your wants can easily be met as there
is plenty to go around.

If you want kind friendships, ask for it. If you want affluence,
ask for it. If you want peace, ask for it. In the asking, make sure

that your actions line up with your requests. If you don't receive what you've asked for, you can stop. You can walk away. You are worthy. You are deserving.

Reflection

What have you wanted but have never made a formal or verbal request of your desires to someone? For example, if you believe you deserve a raise from your employer, ask for one.

Take Action

On a sheet of paper, list three requests that you would like to have fulfilled.

Next to each one, write down the exact date when you will make the request, and to whom.

Also explain how the request will not only benefit you, but also others.

Then, make the requests verbally. If you don't receive the responses you deserve, you have the right to walk away.

76

RESIDING ABOVE THE CLOUDS
● ●

> *Although my body's physical residence is on land,*
> *my mind resides on a mountaintop high above*
> *the clouds free from stress and worry. When it*
> *storms, my body becomes wet and weak, but my*
> *mind remains strong, relaxed, and at peace.*
> —*Shannon Jones*

I WANT TO RESIDE ABOVE THE CLOUDS, EVEN THOUGH MY PHYSICAL
residence is on land. I want to reside far from stress, suffering, and
fear. I want to reside so far up that nothing upsets me. I want to
be so far up that drama no longer exists. Not because it doesn't
exist, but because it doesn't exist for me. Because I choose to give
it no energy.

I want to be so far up that I love those who don't love me back.
So far up that I equally support the blue and the black.

Residing above the clouds gives me clarity of thought, or better
yet, no thought at all. It gives me peace of mind. It's where I have
no skin in the game and where nothing gets under my skin.

I want to be so far up that problems fall away due to a lack of oxygen. Where red blood cells regenerate, giving oxygen to every situation. I want to be so far up that negativity has no charge. Where positivity is in charge. A place where anger is defeated. Where fear is obsolete. A place where only love and kindness are released.

I want to reside above the clouds. I want this to be my permanent residence, no matter the circumstance. I want to reside above the clouds, no matter my physical residence.

Reflection

After reading this expression, did you find your mind at peace?

Do you believe such a place can exist for you?

Take Action

Create a daily intention to live above the clouds, free from stress and worry.

Next, participate in daily activities to align with this intention. Activities may include meditating for thirty minutes a day—fifteen minutes in the morning and fifteen minutes before bedtime.

Prayer and showing gratitude are also great activities to incorporate into your day.

Try establishing and committing to this daily practice to experience peace and mindfulness. Please be patient with the process. As with anything new, it takes time to create a habit and to experience the benefits of these new habits.

77

NATURE'S SOUND BATH MEDITATION

● ●

*Nature created the first sound bath meditation. Where
living things offer the greatest symphonic performance
on earth. Where else but in nature can you enjoy a
show for free while having a great therapy session?*
—*Shannon Jones*

NATURE IS MEDITATION. IT IS A SOUND BATH MEDITATION. IN THE
daytime, the birds sing and the leaves clap. At nighttime, the
katydids, crickets, and locusts perform a nocturnal symphony.
The sounds are clear and harmonious. They clear energy blocks
and aid my parasympathetic nervous system. As I listen to the
rhythmic sounds of nature, stress separates from my body. My
brain waves enter a school zone. My breath begins to follow the
sounds of nature. My mind is being cleansed. My heart is being
repaired. My voice will speak truth and authenticity.

As I am bathed in the sounds of nature, I relinquish all resistance
and the need to control. I let go and let nature do its magic. As I
listen, my mind is wrapped in a cocoon of deep relaxation. The

sounds of nature soothe my aching soul and frayed emotions. This is therapy. This is healing. This is freedom. This is free.

Reflection

When was the last time you communed with nature?

Do you see nature as a source of healing?

Take Action

This week, go outside and be present with nature.

Observe the sounds of nature.

What insects do you hear?

When you go out in nature, close your eyes, and take three deep breaths, breathing in and breathing out slowly.

Try to experience nature for at least thirty minutes. You may notice a sense of peace and oneness with nature. Make this a weekly practice.

78

ILLUSIONS

. . . .

The eyes see what the mind creates.
—Shannon Jones

HOW DO I THRIVE WHEN I'M DETERIORATING?
How do I dream when I have no hope?
How do I laugh when life isn't funny?
How do I reach when I have no arms?
How do I move when I am stationary?

I create an illusion using my senses of what I want to experience. I create an interpretation of the experience that I want to feel until that experience becomes real in my three-dimensional world. I create the illusion in such a way that it feels like I am physically experiencing the experience that I am seeking. Once the brain is convinced that I have already experienced the experience, the mind and body align with what is perceived as real until it becomes real.

If I want to laugh when life is no longer funny, I use my mind to create a scene of humor. In the scene, I am a funny character. As I picture this, I become funny, and my life begins to laugh.

If I want to move when I am stationary, I envision that I am a leaf blowing in the wind, dancing to the beat of the breeze. I picture myself as a leaf that is not only moving but changing with the seasons. As a leaf, I welcome the fall foliage, until my life is filled with motion and vibrant colors.

Reflection

What do you want to experience?

Take Action

Close your eyes and visualize your life as a movie.

Create a movie of the life you really want to have. In this movie, what is the story line? The story line can be something like a life of mediocrity to fulfillment, or sadness to happiness.

Who are the characters? Try to create characters that support your life of satisfaction.

What are you doing in this movie that creates satisfaction?

After you have created the movie from start to finish, take a piece of paper and write out the movie script. Next, look for opportunities where you are already living the movie.

Then, look for opportunities where you can start living the movie.

Lastly, capture the feeling of just the thought of living the movie until you get closer to performing the movie.

79

DON'T TRUST WHAT YOU SEE
••••••••••••••••••••••••••••••••••••

Although your two eyes give you eyesight, your third
eye gives you insight. Insight is like a trusted friend.
—*Shannon Jones*

JUST BECAUSE YOU CAN'T SEE IT DOESN'T MEAN IT DOESN'T EXIST.
Just because you can't touch it doesn't mean it's not yours.

If what you see is not a true reflection of your gifts and talents,
don't trust what you see.

If what you see hasn't caught up to your potential, don't trust
what you see.

If what you see is an unfulfilled life, and you know there is more
to life than what you see, don't trust what you see.

If what you see is not who you are meant to be, don't trust what
you see.

If what you see isn't congruent to the best version of yourself,
don't trust what you see.

If what you see is dull, and you were born to shine, don't trust what you see.

If what you see are roadblocks, and you know there's got to be an outlet, don't trust what you see.

Don't trust what you see. Trust what you know. If you don't know, trust the one who does.

Reflection

What do you see?

Is what you see what you want to see?

Take Action

What you see is not always what is. Think back to a time when what you saw was not the real story. Analyze what you saw versus what was.

What are some lessons that you can bring forward to right now to help you trust what you know, if what you know is not what you see?

Also, analyze *why* what you are seeing in your life does not reflect what you want or who you are. There may be blocks that need to be removed before you can move forward.

80

ALL THERE IS TO KNOW
•••••••••••••••••••••••••••••••••••

You will know me by the music I listen to,
the books I read, and the company I keep.
—*Shannon Jones*

WE MAY NEVER BE PEN PALS. WE MAY NEVER BE LUNCHMATES. I may never get invited to your house for dinner. We may never spend long nights on the phone. We may never sit on an airplane and chat like perfect strangers. We may never bump into each other at the gym. We may never attend a yoga class together. We may never know the same people.

But if you know the type of music I listen to, you know me—even if my type of music doesn't make you groove. Because my type of music fuels my soul to brighten yours.

If you know the genre of books I read, you know me—even if the books I read aren't your type. Because the books I read calm my mind so I can help you find solace.

If you know the company I keep, you know me—even if we don't share the same company. Because the company I keep shows kindness so that I can give it to you.

Although you don't know me, if you know the music I listen to, the books I read, and the company I keep, *you know me.*

Reflection

Does the music that you listen to reflect kindness, love, and peace?

Does what you read fuel your mind positively? What are you reading?

Your friends are a reflection of you. What are they reflecting?

Take Action

The next time you listen to music, create awareness of what you are listening to. What is the message? Is it a message of kindness, love, and peace, or is it full of destruction and violence?

What are the last three books you've read? Are you better for reading them?

What are your friends like? Are they honest, kind, compassionate, and loving?

81

I CHOOSE MY "I'M TOO'S"
• •

> *Life is a series of combined sentences woven*
> *together to create a story. The best stories*
> *are formed when the storyteller becomes fully*
> *aware of who they are, to begin to change their*
> *sentences and eventually their entire story.*
> —*Shannon Jones*

I'M TOO OLD TO START A BUSINESS.

I'm too young to run a business.

I'm too underqualified to be best qualified.

I'm too late to be considered.

I'm too early to take action.

I'm too simple to find a solution.

I'm too complicated to simplify the equation.

I'm too big to fit the mold.

I'm too small to be in charge.

I'm too irrelevant to be taken seriously.

I'm too uneducated to train others.

I'm too inexperienced to know what I want.

I'm too safe to take risks.

I'm too risky to make good investments.

Don't give energy to "I'm too's" that tear down and not build up. Even if the "I'm too's" are "true" for you, it doesn't mean they are "true."

Instead, give energy to:

I'm too gifted to not gift the world.
I'm too talented to let my talents lie dormant.
I'm too deserving to not deserve the best.
I'm too tenacious to accept defeat.
I'm too significant to be overlooked.
I'm too blessed to be cursed.
I'm too valued to be worth nothing.
I'm too wise to be bothered with foolish things.
I'm too considerate to not be considered.
I'm too good to be treated badly.
I'm too loving to not be loved.
I'm too hopeful to live my life in despair.

I decide to choose my "I'm too's."

Reflection

What "I'm too's" have you told yourself?

Are these "I'm too's" negative and limiting, or positive and empowering?

Take Action

These "I'm too's" not only form our beliefs but they *are* our beliefs. What we put our attention on expands. Therefore, you are either expanding negatively or expanding positively. These beliefs show up in our lives daily and rob us of a more fulfilling life. For example, if you have told yourself that you are not good enough, you will likely not embrace opportunities because you have convinced yourself that you are not deserving.

Take a sheet of paper and fold it in half. On the left side write a list of limiting "I'm too's" that you have reiterated to yourself. On the right side of the paper, write the empowering "I'm too's" that you want to manifest in your life.

Now review and compare both lists. The purpose of this exercise is to bring awareness to your limiting beliefs so that you can start to change your sentences, and ultimately, your story.

82

OUR NEEDS ARE THE SAME, JUST IN DIFFERENT FORMS

•••••••••••••••••••••••••••••••••••••••

> *Human needs are like homophones. They*
> *sound the same but are just spelled differently.*
> *After all, we all want to be appreciated, to be*
> *respected, and to know that we matter.*
> —*Shannon Jones*

YOU NEED WATER.
I need H_2O.
You need carbohydrates.
I need sugars and starches.
You need proteins and fats.
I need meats and oils.
You need affection.
I need direction.
You need a little of this.
I need a little of that.
You need to be wanted.
I need to be needed.
You need to be admired.

I need to be inspired.
You need to be pursued.
I need to be debuted.
You need to be heard.
I need to be learned.

To be learned, you must be heard. The person who is admired also inspires. When it all boils down, we all want the same things. We want to be appreciated, to be respected, and to know that we matter.

Reflection

How does it make you feel when you are appreciated, respected, and know that you matter?

Who makes you feel appreciated, respected, and like you matter?

Who do you appreciate, respect, and show that they matter?

Take Action

Think of a person who you don't get along with. This could be a coworker, partner, etc.

This week, look for similarities that the two of you share. If it's difficult to find similarities, remember that you each want to be appreciated, to be respected, and to know that you matter. These are the greatest similarities of humankind.

More often than not, our disagreements stem from our heightened awareness of our differences. As we look for similarities, many of these differences will subside.

83

FIND OR CREATE
• •

Find what's hidden, create what doesn't exist.
—Shannon Jones

HOW DOES A FLOWER PIERCE THROUGH A CRACKED CONCRETE sidewalk? How does a newborn pierce through the birth canal? How does a ray of sunlight pierce through the clouds?

The flower takes advantage of the hidden moisture under the earth and concrete, then finds a crack in the sidewalk and barrels through to display its beauty and strength.

The newborn travels through the birth canal on an unknown journey, provoking a massive expansion—an opening, creating a miracle.

The crepuscular ray finds the gap in the clouds to showcase its radiant sunlight.

Each of these phenomena continuously find or create an opening or space. You have the ability and creativity to find what's hidden and to create what doesn't exist.

If you can't buy it, make it.
If it's not produced, grow it.
If you can't occupy it, build it.
If it doesn't exist, invent it.
If you can't touch it, imagine it.

If they won't hire you, hire yourself.
If they won't invest in you, invest in yourself.
If your hands are tied, use your feet.
If the bank says no, know there is at least one that will say yes.

Find, create, look, or make.

Reflection

What can you find or create?

Take Action

Starting today, assess three situations in your life that have potential to help you meet your goals. In your assessment, look for hidden opportunities that you may have overlooked in the past. This may take the form of being open to friendships which could evolve into a business partnership. It may take the form of a request from a coworker or someone seeking your help on a project that comes very easily to you. Picture this activity as a connect-the-dots puzzle. Now go hunt for clues to see a clearer picture of what you can find, create, look, or make.

84

MY NEEDS MUST
TAKE PRIORITY

•••••••••••••••••••••••••••••••••••••

I refuse to allow your wants to come before my needs.
—*Shannon Jones*

I WANT TO GIVE YOU MORE, BUT NOT AT THE EXPENSE OF GIVING me less.

I have $100 in my emotional bank account.

You asked for $5, which I gladly gave to help you strive.

You demanded $10, which I gave in the form of a listening ear. I gave knowing that when I need to talk, you won't give me your ear to hear.

$20 was withdrawn in a heated debate. All I was saying was that I needed you to relate. Oh, how I wished we could've been soulmates.

Now you want $25 to help support your career. I give knowing that your wants are insincere.

You desire another $20 for a new business enterprise. I give because I don't want to be criticized.

$10 are withdrawn from years of hurt and pain. I can't figure out how you can treat me with so much disdain. It's really inhumane.

I have $10 left. Now you want some advice. Oh, that's why you're being so nice. What I give you for free, I charge others' a price.

I'm all spent. I have nothing left. I don't know why I didn't prioritize myself. Although a few deposits were made into my account, so much more was taken out.

I now have a negative balance. I'm emotionally bankrupt. I'm now challenging myself to not allow anyone's wants to come before my needs.

Reflection

On a scale from one to ten, with ten signifying the most, how much do you have in your emotional bank account?

Are you emotionally bankrupt?

Take Action

On a sheet of paper, list five of your needs that you refuse to sacrifice.

How committed are you to honoring these items daily or weekly?

If one of your top five items is that you need alone time, make an appointment with yourself. Put it on your calendar and make sure that your close family members and friends are aware of your unavailability. If travel is one of your top priorities, you may have to negotiate with yourself to find a timeline that works for you while balancing your budget and commitments.

Printed in the United States
by Baker & Taylor Publisher Services

.